FEB 2002

THE LESSONS OF TERROR

THE LESSONS OF
TERROR

**A HISTORY OF WARFARE AGAINST CIVILIANS:
WHY IT HAS ALWAYS FAILED AND WHY IT WILL FAIL AGAIN**

CALEB CARR

RANDOM HOUSE
NEW YORK

Copyright © 2002 by Caleb Carr

All rights reserved under International and Pan-American
Copyright Conventions. Published in the United States
by Random House, Inc., New York, and simultaneously in
Canada by Random House of Canada Limited, Toronto.

RANDOM HOUSE and colophon are registered
trademarks of Random House, Inc.

ISBN 0-375-50843-0

Random House website address: www.atrandom.com

Printed in the United States of America on acid-free paper

24689753

First Edition

Book design by Casey Hampton

THIS BOOK IS DEDICATED TO

ANN GODOFF

Friend and Editor,
who understood from the beginning
how important this project was to its author

CONTENTS

If a man is slain unjustly, his heir shall be entitled to satisfaction. But let him not carry his vengeance to excess, for his victim is sure to be assisted and avenged.

—THE KORAN, 17:33

If an unjust and rapacious conqueror subdues a nation, and forces her to accept hard, ignominious, and insupportable conditions, necessity obliges her to submit: but this apparent tranquility is not a peace; it is an oppression which she endures only so long as she wants the means of shaking it off, and against which men of spirit arise on the first favorable opportunity.

—EMMERICH DE VATTEL, *The Law of Nations*

ACKNOWLEDGMENTS

The ideas contained in this book first took written form in an article I published in 1996 in *The World Policy Journal,* which at the time was under the stewardship of my friend and mentor James Chace. There is little of value in my life that has not been affected by James's wise counsel, although the opinions expressed herein are most certainly mine alone.

My agent, Suzanne Gluck, along with her husband, Tom Dyja, who supplied a title, were staunch supporters of this undertaking from the start, as indeed they have always been.

In the event that the dedication of this volume is in any way ambiguous, allow me to add that Ann Godoff has consistently supported not only the most popular of my undertakings, but those that are most personally important to me; and for that, as well as for her continued friendship, I am deeply grateful.

Also at Random House, I would like to thank Sunshine Lucas, Timothy Mennel, Benjamin Dreyer, James Danly, Casey Hampton, Sarah D'Imperio, Tom Perry, and the enormously talented Andy Carpenter. Melissa Strickland and Pam de Montmorency provided swift expert research assistance, without which this work would not have been a practical proposition; to them, and to the rest of the remarkable ladies at the Battery Park Research Institute, I offer the deepest affection and appreciation.

My conversations with Ezequiel Viñao, who shared the results of his own extensive research as well as his unique insights, were vital.

Oren Jacoby and Jennifer Maguire provided encouragement early on, and I thank them.

My old and trusted friend Rob Cowley agreed to study the manuscript and make suggestions. Once again, no one should infer the opinions expressed herein are anyone's but my own; but being able to benefit from the advice of such learned and good-hearted colleagues has always been an invaluable advantage.

This was a particularly tough schedule to meet; and for their help with vital daily details, I thank my family, as well as Arnie Kellar, photographer William von Hartz, Ellen Blain, Tom Pivinski, Perrin Wright, and Bruce Yaffe, M.D. extraordinary.

THE LESSONS OF TERROR

PROLOGUE

To be emblematic of our age is to bear an evil burden. The twentieth century, scarcely finished, will be remembered as much for its succession of wars and genocides as it will for anything else; and sadly the dawn of the new millennium has brought no end to this horrifying tradition. The first year of the twenty-first century produced images that will likely identify the decade, if not the generation, to come: commercial aircraft, hijacked by agents of extremism, slamming into crowded, unprotected office buildings, bringing about the collapse of those structures and the deaths of thousands of people.

How can we have come to this? How can we have reached a moment in history when men professing to be soldiers serving a cause are capable not only of committing such atrocities but of calling them acts of war?

In this era of ethnic and religious strife we know only

too well that human conflict is often inexplicably savage; and yet there were and remain questions about the events of September 11, 2001, that seem to defy even our sadly overdeveloped inurement to horror. The cacophony produced by media sensationalists and television talking heads, a continuous aspect of daily life since the attacks, has done nothing more than crystallize these basic questions, which have gone on to embed themselves in the minds of citizens in every country facing the threat of what has, over the last generation, become known as "international terrorism." As the initial assaults in New York, Washington, and Pennsylvania have led to countermeasures and then, inevitably, to further outrages, these deep and troublesome queries have continued to work their way into the vulnerable fiber of the public psyche— for these are questions that do not admit of sound-bite solutions, that do not fade even as we see the architects of the massacres arrested, attacked, and killed:

How can we, how can human civilization, possibly have reached such a point?

The immediate causes of the current crisis have been discussed to such a numbing extent that they have attained for many people a somewhat rote quality: again and again stories are disseminated about the grievances and fanaticism of extremists from nations in the Middle East and Asia, about the morally ambiguous economic expansionism of the West, and about the inevitable clash between the two sides' religions, cultures, and wildly conflicting conceptions of how people should live. Yet these never-ending and finally overwhelming dissections seem somehow unequal to the events we are living through, never attaining commensurate scope or magnitude.

There is nothing inappropriate about this confusion, this sense of disconnection between lived facts and received commentary. Relatively few people alive today can recall with more than childhood vagueness the last time that civilization faced such a truly epochal moment; and of those few who are old enough to have participated in the struggle against fascism and totalitarianism during the middle of the twentieth century, there are almost certainly none who are actively making executive decisions about the content of television programming or newspaper and magazine articles. Even if there were, television, newspapers, and magazines cannot supply the proper context for studies of what we are experiencing, since they are at best shortsighted records of recent happenings and at worst mere entertainment disguised as thought. Epochal moments belong rightly to history, and it is history that holds the only hope of providing an understanding of the twisted road that has brought us to this frightening pass.

This brief book is intended to provide an introduction to the historical roots of modern international terrorism by placing that phenomenon squarely within the discipline of military history, rather than political science or sociology. It will be proposed that what has to date been viewed and treated as a uniquely modern problem is in fact the current stage in a violent evolution whose origins extend as far back as does human conflict itself: *terrorism, in other words, is simply the contemporary name given to, and the modern permutation of, warfare deliberately waged against civilians with the purpose of destroying their will to support either leaders or policies that the agents of such violence find objectionable.*

Bloodshed of this kind is quite distinct from what many now label (often with utter disingenuousness) "collateral damage"—that is, accidental casualties inflicted on civilians by warring military units. Yet like collateral damage, deliberate warfare against civilians has always been with us and cannot be truly understood out of context. Any examination of its historical origins must therefore rest on numerous specific precedents if it is to contribute to a deeper and more productive discussion of our present crisis. That such discussion continues to be necessary at all levels of society, regardless of the day-to-day development of events and policies that affect particular aspects of our current predicament, is indicated by a difficult but ongoing problem: although terrorists themselves must bear the principal culpability for their activities, violent and otherwise, citizens and leaders of the nations and communities in which they have chosen to create their

particular form of hell cannot completely escape responsibility, for we have either misunderstood or ignored both
the origins and nature of the threat to an extent sufficient
to have made the work of its perpetrators far easier.

To contend as much, in the light of recent events,
smacks dangerously of blaming the victim; yet when we
understand just how this form of violence fits into the
record of human conflict, we will see that such terms as
victim and *perpetrator* attain altered definitions—as, indeed, does the word *terrorism* itself.

Over the past forty years, American and other world
leaders have generally identified international terrorism
(as distinct from *domestic* terrorism, which falls outside
the scope of this study) as a type of crime, in an effort to
rally global indignation against the agents of such mayhem and deny them the more respected status of actual
soldiers. Even since the September 11 attacks caused
many such leaders to acknowledge a global "war" against
terrorists, for example, the actions of those terrorists have
been described more often as "criminal" than as "belligerent." And to be sure, before they developed the tactic of
turning commercial airplanes into ballistic missiles, terrorists' typical behavior (whether assassination, kidnapping, or bombing) was often indistinguishable from that
of common criminals. In addition, terrorist causes fre-
quently attracted—and still do attract—individuals who
simply use philosophical or political rationalizations to

veil their more fundamental greed and bloodlust: as has been noted of late, terrorist organizations—with their money laundering, drug dealing, and forgery experts—bear more than a passing resemblance to the families of organized crime.

Yet there has always been a central problem with insisting that terrorists are essentially criminals: such categorization generally limits to reactive and defensive measures the range of responses that the American and other governments can justifiably employ. During most of the Clinton administration's eight years, for example, despite the fact that the natures and purposes of such global terrorist organizations as Osama bin Laden's Al Qaeda were well-known, almost all federal funds for antiterrorist efforts were targeted at detective and intelligence work, while preemptive military strikes against terrorist leaders, networks, or bases were ignored. (Clinton's most significant military move against terrorism, the bombings of Afghanistan and Sudan that followed terrorist attacks on U.S. embassies in Africa in 1998, were wholly reactive and completely predictable, to say nothing of utterly ineffective.) In the present crisis, George W. Bush's administration, rather than take full advantage of the rules that typically govern a state of war, has taken limited advantage only of the *weapons* of war: strategically, it early on accepted the demand of many nations that America legally "prove" its case against Al Qaeda, as if the struggle against terrorism were being conducted in some open-air international courtroom, rather than on the battlefields of New York, Pennsylvania, Washington, Afghanistan, and dozens of lower-profile sites.

In other words, our leaders (and we as their citizens) have in the past been, and in disturbing numbers remain, prepared to treat terrorists as being on a par with smugglers, drug traffickers, or, at most, some kind of political mafiosi, rather than what they have in fact been for almost half a century: organized, highly trained, hugely destructive paramilitary units that were and are conducting offensive campaigns against a variety of nations and social systems. In truth, international terrorism has always been what its perpetrators have so often insisted: a form of warfare. And although American leaders and the international media were more than willing after the September 11 attacks to announce that the United States was in fact at war, a truly unified, comprehensive and resolute military strategy for conducting this war was slow in formulation and has proved difficult to maintain. Confusion and arguments over terms and concepts, goals and strategies, have hampered the prosecution of America's response from the start.

The costs of this confusion are apparent, the reasons behind it less so. Yet in a very real sense they center on one consideration above all: the status and nature of the enemy who has brought unprecedented death and destruction to our shores. Not just as Westerners but as human beings, we tend to ascribe a certain prejudicial nobility to the terms *soldier* and *warrior*. We have no wish to recognize such a quality in or bestow such titles on men and women who deliberately set out to victimize average citizens, noncombatants whose only reliable means of influencing the policies of their leaders is the occasional vote or the even more infrequent rebellion. Yet the purposeful targeting of civilians is nothing new in warfare—in fact it is, as said, as old as warfare itself—and the world has been more than willing to accord the status of "soldiers" to some of its most vicious practitioners. This book, therefore, is not a history of fringe groups or obscure cults. It is the tale of a type of war that has been practiced at one time or another by every nation on earth—including, all too often, the United States.

Indeed, several of the most fabled heroes of the American Civil War—Thomas "Stonewall" Jackson, William Tecumseh Sherman, and others—were responsible for the systemization and legitimization of what at the time was viewed as an extreme (though nonetheless common) military tactic. Nor is the list of great historical figures who fit the definition of *terrorist*—that is, someone who deliberately attacks civilians in order to effect a change in both the support of those civilians for their leaders and the policies of those leaders themselves—

limited to strictly military or paramilitary figures: the Roman emperor Augustus, France's King Louis XIV, Germany's Otto von Bismarck, and the American team of Richard Nixon and Henry Kissinger are but a few of the statesmen who helped perpetuate the practice.

All such figures were in fact "soldiers," whether they considered themselves such or not. They were perhaps not soldiers in the narrow, Western, and largely ephemeral terms of the Geneva protocols of the early twentieth century, but they were indeed soldiers in the most primal, universal, and enduring sense, as were the hijackers who flew airliners into the World Trade Center and the Pentagon. One can refuse to call such people an army, if one wishes; yet they are organized as an army, and certainly they conduct themselves as an army, giving and taking secret orders to attack their enemies with a variety of tactics that serve one overarching strategy: terror.

But perhaps the most significant thing that the terrorists of today share with those who practiced warfare against civilians in earlier times is an abiding inability to see that the strategy of terror is a spectacularly failed one. Surprising and difficult as it may be to accept that what we call terrorism is in fact a form of warfare, it may be even more surprising and difficult—particularly given that we are in the midst of a war with terrorists—to understand that it is a form that has never succeeded. It is from this discovery, however, that we must today take both our greatest hope and our sternest warning. Warfare against civilians, whether inspired by hatred, revenge, greed, or political and psychological insecurity, has been one of the most ultimately self-defeating tactics in all of military history—indeed, it would be difficult to think of one more inimical to its various practitioners' causes. And yet those same imperatives—hatred, revenge, greed, and insecurity—have driven nations and factions both great and small to the strategy of terror and the tactic of waging war on civilians time and time again. Some parts of the world, in fact, have become so locked into the cycle of outrages and reprisals against civilians that their histories comprise little else. But out of all this bloody confusion one clear assertion repeatedly presents itself: the nation or faction that resorts to warfare against civilians most quickly, most often, and most viciously is the nation or faction most likely to see its interests frustrated and, in many cases, its existence terminated.

In the ensuing chapters and examples, we will see this surprising conclusion illustrated in many historical epochs going back to that of the Roman republic, and from this sad saga we can draw a second critical conclusion. By defining *terrorism* as *war,* we have already implied that attacks against civilians can be appropriately met only by military action (though this is not to say that military action should not be augmented by intelligence and criminological work); but the nature of that military action is as important as its undertaking. And in considering what that nature should be, we come upon another historical lesson as apparent as it has been ignored: warfare against civilians must never be answered in kind. For as failed a tactic as such warfare has been, reprisals similarly directed at civilians have been even more so—particularly when they have exceeded the original assault in scope.

The successful answer to the terrorist threat, then, lies not in repeated analyses of individual contemporary terrorist movements, nor in legalistic attempts to condemn their behavior in courts of international law, nor in reactionary policies and actions that punish civilian populations as much as the terrorists who operate from among them. Rather, it lies in the formulation of a comprehensive, progressive strategy that can address all terrorist threats with the only coercive measures that have ever affected or moderated terrorist (or any other military or paramilitary) behavior: preemptive military offensives aimed at making not only terrorists but the states that harbor, supply, and otherwise assist them experience the same perpetual insecurity that they attempt to make their victims feel. The methods must be different, of course, for, as stated, terror must never be answered with terror; but war can *only* be answered with war, and it is incumbent on us to devise a style of war more imaginative, more decisive, and yet more humane than anything terrorists can contrive. Such a strategy does indeed exist; but it cannot be delineated without first tracing both the long history of warfare against civilians that has produced the present problem of terrorism in the first place, as well as the saga of those efforts that have been made in the past to address and curtail that savage tradition.

In other words, military history alone can teach us the lessons that will solve the dilemma of modern international terrorism. These lessons are not necessarily new; they have, in many cases, been apparent for centuries and to many previous generations of perceptive leaders. Yet most of these leaders have been unable to resist the temptation to make war against civilians, no matter how threatening to their own interests that indulgence may ultimately have proved to have been—for terror's lure as a seemingly quick and gratifying solution is a powerful one. It is by no means the contention of this book, then, that we have reached a point in history where warfare against civilians might suddenly become morally and militarily obsolete. Nor will this overview assert that the tactics of terror can be defeated quickly: as a rule the process of frustrating them is generational in duration and broad in scope. What this study *can* claim, however, is that whenever and wherever such tactics have been indulged, they have been and are still destined to ultimately fail: this is the central lesson to be learned, and the chief cause of

hope that can be taken, from the often troubling history
that fills the following pages.

A final note: when I first presented the core of these
ideas half a decade ago, many experts on terrorism whose
work I have long respected pronounced that I was over-
reacting to the menace then at hand by advocating "the
liberal use of military force" and "elucidating a war paradigm." I have always confessed to a less than perfect understanding of what that last phrase might mean; but if
the implication was that I was recommending that
Americans do what their enemies had long been doing—
making war with all the means at their disposal—then I
accept the criticism and suggest that it is the terrorists
who first "elucidated" such a "paradigm." At any rate,
that the dangers of terrorism are continuing to grow I
hold as presently irrefutable. Despite our current military
efforts, the core terrorist threats—biological, chemical,
and even nuclear warfare, suicide bombings and attacks,
and still more airplane hijackings, along with the complex
programs of state sponsorship necessary to prepare for
such actions—remain largely unaddressed at their international roots, whatever our successes against specific
groups or individuals. For many years, we ignored these
dangers or, worse yet, tried to react to them by addressing
the motivations and goals of their agents rather than their
behavior. But today, responding to terrorism is not a mat-

ter for sociological study or negotiation: terrorists are no longer holding guns to our heads and making demands— they are pulling triggers without discussion or warning. Continued and, in all likelihood, escalated military action will be the only remedy for this problem. Terrorism will be eradicated not when we come to some sort of accommodation with its agents, nor when we physically destroy them, but rather when it is perceived as a strategy and a behavior that yields nothing save eventual defeat for those causes that inspire it. (After all, even suicidal terrorists, though they care nothing for their own lives or the lives of others, venerate their cause.) History holds the key to this momentous transformation from world scourge to tactical and behavioral relic; and so it is to history that we must now turn.

CHAPTER ONE

A CATASTROPHE, NOT A CURE

Long before the deliberate military targeting of civilians as a method of affecting the political behavior of nations and leaders came to be called *terrorism,* the tactic had a host of other names. From the time of the Roman republic to the late eighteenth century, for example, the phrase that was most often used was *destructive war.* The Romans themselves often used the phrase *punitive war,* although strictly speaking punitive expeditions and raids were only a part of destructive war. For while many Roman military campaigns were indeed undertaken as punishment for treachery or rebellion, other destructive actions sprang out of the simple desire to impress newly conquered peoples with the fearsome might of Rome, and thereby (or so it was hoped) undercut any support for indigenous leaders. In addition, there was a pressing need to allow the famous Roman legions, who were infamously underpaid, to plunder and rape as a reward for their almost inhuman steadiness in the heat of battle. The example of Rome incorporates nearly every possible permutation of warfare against civilians: in this as in so many things, antiquity's greatest state provided a remarkably complete set of precedents for many later Western republics and empires.

The Romans knew only one way to fight—with relentless yet disciplined ferocity—but they eventually devised several ways to deal with the peace that ensued. The first and most successful was inclusive in nature: the peoples of conquered provinces could, if they agreed to abide by Roman authority and law, aspire to become citizens of the republic (and later the empire). Indeed, some new subjects, particularly merchants and other civic leaders, could achieve the status quite quickly. Even slaves could aspire to citizenship, for early on the Romans had devised a remarkable system of manumission, providing multiple avenues by which slaves could escape the hopelessness of unending bondage (and the tendency toward rebellion that hopelessness often breeds) by attempting to earn, buy, or be granted first freedom and then actual citizenship. Freedmen played an important part in Roman history (more than one emperor was saved by a loyal freedman); and on the whole, these complementary policies— granting citizenship to conquered peoples and offering slaves the hope of manumission—may safely be called the central domestic foundation on which the near millennium of Roman hegemony rested.

But like so many empires and great powers that followed them, the Romans also engaged in more avaricious, less benevolent policies that many times came close to undoing all the security and stability built up by their genius. First among these was a pronounced taste for revenge against enemies who were perceived as intractable or treacherous—the most famous example of such mortal enemies being the Carthaginian empire of the late third century B.C.E. and its leader, Hannibal. The long years of struggle against Hannibal—whose raids and campaigns throughout Italy bred both bloodthirsty hatred and a powerful sense of vulnerability in his opponents—eventually led the Romans, when they finally did occupy Carthage more than fifty years later, to not only sack but utterly destroy the city. And although they soon built their own urban center atop the ruins, the experience gave apparent validation to an already unfortunate, even fatal, tendency in both the Roman military and its masters in the Senate.

The razing of Carthage had been that rarest of things in a nation's experience: the utter eradication not only of the enemy's home but of many if not most of his people as well: men, women, children, even the elderly. It was the epitome of destructive war, and the Romans not only revered the memory of it but attempted at various times to repeat it. In so doing, they planted at least a few of the seeds of their own eventual downfall: for, along with being rare, the destruction of Carthage would prove beyond replication. Yet the Roman taste for vicious destructive war that the Carthaginian experience sharpened grew stronger with each new generation, until it became powerful enough to threaten the stability that the empire's brilliant system of citizenship and manumission had made seem so unshakable.

Throughout the remainder of its history, Rome was dominated by the tension between these two imperatives: on the one hand, the enlightened desire to be an inclusive empire built not on destructive war but on forceful economic and political expansion; and on the other, the violent compulsion—bred in the army but fed by romantic notions of war popular among all Roman citizens—to be a chauvinistic, plundering state that simply took whatever it wanted from whoever had it. Rome's metamorphosis into an empire just before the birth of Christ tilted the scales alarmingly but inevitably in favor of the second of these two conceptions, despite the efforts of several perspicacious emperors to prevent such a shift. For, with the eclipse of the Senate as the critical arm of government, the numerous political factions vying for control of the state and balancing one another's ambitions gave way to a very limited number of imperial factions; and when power was being contested by just a few people who were neither elected nor answerable to the citizenry, the army became the single most important force in the maintenance of power. And it was the army that had always looked to destructive war, first, as a means with which to set grim examples for politically rebellious subjects, second, to avenge any defeats and betrayals it sustained, and lastly, as a way to augment the comparatively meager pay that soldiers received and sate their appetites during campaigning.

It is not surprising, then, that Rome's imperial centuries were characterized not only by more severe versions of the types of warfare against civilians that had been a hallmark of military activity during the republic, but by new and astoundingly savage—as well as often gratuitous—destructive tactics. It has, of course, been argued (not least by the Romans themselves) that the empire was fighting barbarian tribes, and that its forces needed to adopt the tactics of their enemies if they hoped to succeed. (Similar arguments have often been employed by various individuals and groups during the contemporary war against terrorism.) But quite apart from the fact that the Romans were fighting not only barbarian tribes but established, civilized societies such as the Jewish communities located throughout what we now call the Middle East, Roman leaders had already had ample time and experience to learn the speciousness of this reasoning. In the first place, punitive and destructive war against the nonwarrior members of any group that was not Roman ("barbarian" tribe or no) only led to the creation of generations of anti-Roman sentiment within that group. Then, too, Rome was rarely at war with entire tribes so much as with those charismatic leaders that occasionally surfaced to lead their peoples in rebellion—peoples who, again, had often been made restive by Roman cruelty.

In other words, we can detect in the example of Rome the most essential truth about warfare against civilians: that when waged without provocation it usually brings on retaliation in kind, and when turned to for retaliatory purposes it only perpetuates a cycle of revenge and outrage that can go on for generations. Therefore it should be avoided in both its forms—initial and reactive—for, again, those nations and peoples who indulge in warfare against civilians to the greatest extent will ultimately see their people and their interests suffer to a similar degree. Rome's greatest conquests were not achieved *because* of the depredations that occurred either to keep troublesome subjects obedient or after battles and sieges had been won; they were achieved *despite* those depredations and because the promise of inclusion in the society and infrastructure of Rome was too attractive for most people to refuse. The cruelties inflicted by the Roman army achieved only the creation and perpetuation of underlying bitterness, which could simmer and finally boil over into open support for rebellious leaders who urged a return to more traditional tribal societies.

There is an irony concerning most of those rebel leaders that also holds enormous implications for our present experience: the most dangerous and effective of them were men who had been trained by Rome itself, usually in the ranks and often in the officer corps of the legions. It was this training that enabled them to organize their warriors into disciplined units capable of combating the Romans with their own methods. The clear lesson here is one that has stood the test of countless brutal struggles over the ages: a nation must never think that it can use (and especially train) the agents of terror when convenient and then be rid of them when they are no longer needed. For just as meeting the tactics of terror in kind will only perpetuate the cycle of terrorist violence, so making use of terror's practitioners to meet the exigencies of a momentary political or military crisis will almost certainly result in those practitioners turning against their supposed allies and masters once the common enemy has been defeated. In the imperial era, as warfare became less fashionable among young Romans, Rome increasingly depended on barbarian troops for defense: Roman rulers' subsequent and numerous unfortunate experiences with foreign-born but Roman-trained soldiers who turned against the empire should have taught them this lesson many times over. Yet those same rulers continued not only to train such men but to put them into positions where they were capable of doing great harm.

One example of all these problematic practices and results stands out in Roman history, perhaps because of how clearly, even chillingly, its central events presaged the breakup of the empire some four hundred years later. During the reign of Augustus it was decided that Rome should try to extend its sway over the tribes east of the Rhine River, in the province of Germania; this, despite the fact that the great Julius Caesar himself (whose famous conquest of Gaul had been quickly solidified by his shrewd award of citizenship to the conquered peoples of the province) had always maintained that the Rhine marked the dividing line between tribes that could be safely absorbed into the empire and those that could not. But glory and loot, those habitual Roman imperatives of conquest (Germania held no strategic value), called Augustus and his armies across the river. When they met stiff resistance from the German tribes, they answered with assaults that were stiffer still; and by the time a Roman province had been formally established, there were many villages and tribes that had good reason to hate their new rulers. True, the advantages of Roman citizenship and the policy of manumission won many over; but the memory of crucified and dismembered bodies and the violations of German women, along with the arrival of a strange new pantheon of gods, ultimately had a much more lasting effect on the Germanic tribes.

In the year 9, the extent to which the seeming peace in Germania was actually a mask—a mask that more and more Germans found it onerous to wear—became fully apparent. For three years, the empire had been grappling with an uprising in Pannonia, east of Italy. Legion after legion had been devoted to the undertaking, forcing Augustus to free large numbers of slaves for induction into the army. At precisely this moment of weakness the governor of newly Roman Germania, Publius Quinctilius Varus, got wind of similar unrest in his own province. He immediately mustered every man he could and marched off to quash the rebellion—unaware as yet that the uprising involved large numbers of his own soldiers (German tribesmen who had supposedly been absorbed into the empire) and was being led by one of his own lieutenants, a German commander of auxiliary troops called Arminius.

All the elements demonstrating the wrongheadedness, to say nothing of the immorality, of ever having waged destructive war against civilians now came into play. Arminius, who had studied Roman tactics while participating in the earlier Pannonian campaign, was immensely charismatic, and much of his authority within the German tribes was based on his appeals to the fundamentals of native German paganism. Above all, he called tribesmen to his cause by renouncing the Roman way of war. He intended to vent his wrath, he said, only on Roman fighting troops, not women, children, and the aged, as the Romans did. Deserting his post in Varus's army soon after the governor's expedition got under way, Arminius directed his men to lead the enemy into the difficult terrain in the vicinity of the Teutoburg Forest, and then they launched a series of ambushes. Varus—panicking when he realized the extent of the trap—killed himself, after which what was left of the three legions he had been leading were slaughtered to a man.

The incident sent a shock wave through the empire; indeed, it may well have hastened the aging, ailing Augustus's death. (The emperor became dementedly obsessed with the defeat and was more than once found wandering unshaven about his palace, beating his head against walls and demanding that Varus return his lost legions.) Soon after Augustus did die, his dour, severe successor, Tiberius, dispatched troops under a more popular member of the imperial family, the handsome young Germanicus, to put down Arminius's rebellion. This process was to take a decade and be conducted with typical Roman ferocity. So great was the extent of the horror that Germanicus himself, after observing his men's slaughter of some of the former Roman soldiers who had rebelled with Arminius, declared, "This is no cure; it is a catastrophe!"

More telling still was Arminius's own defense of his

actions: "My fighting has been open, not treacherous," he told his people, "and it has been against armed men and not pregnant women." Whether or not this was completely true, it was certainly what the Germans wanted to hear, as was Arminius's next claim: "The groves of Germany still display the Roman Eagles and standards which I hung there in honor of the gods of our fathers." He went on to mock the fact that Augustus had been declared a god in Rome, deriding those who had "a human being to worship!" "Other countries," he went on, "unacquainted with Roman rule, have not known its impositions or its punishments. We have known them—and got rid of them!" Telling his followers that if they preferred their own country, their families, "and the old ways to settlement under tyrants abroad," they must continue to follow him, Arminius held out for longer than most who rose up to challenge Roman hegemony; and his followers paid a commensurately more horrifying price when they were subdued.

Yet when the victorious Romans departed Germany after quashing Arminius's rebellion, it was for good: they never attempted to reestablish a formal province east of the Rhine. During the generations that followed, however, the memory of their presence evolved into the stuff of hateful legend among German tribes. Having created their own worst enemy in the brutal school of the Roman army—and, on a larger scale, having constructed a heterogenous society into which even hostile foreigners could blend unnoticed—the Romans had been shaken badly by the massacre in the Teutoburg Forest; and the extent of their insecurity was reflected in the severity of their response.

Had the Romans thought more clearly and calmly, however, they would have realized that the elimination of Arminius alone through assassination—a tactic by no means unacceptable to Roman morality and society—would have taken the wind out of the rebellion. The task would have been a difficult one, since Arminius did not reveal his treachery until the rebellion was under way; but assassination had been a successful tactic in quelling a number of other uprisings, being as such movements—then as today—tended to be organized by and around charismatic leaders who were difficult to replace and who did not tend to surround themselves with characters of equal talent, who might become rivals. Thus when the leader was eliminated, the movement generally withered, a fact that has not been adequately appreciated during our own years of struggle against modern terrorism. Then, too, it should not have been difficult for the Romans to see, given their experiences in other provinces, that large-scale, destructive war against whole German communities would only breed new generations of tribesmen who despised the very idea of Rome. Later, in at-

tempting to deal with similar conflicts, the Romans came
to rely increasingly on more limited and focused tactics,
often with success; but by then the damage had been
done. Centuries of hurling their might against not only
foreign armies but foreign civilians had undermined the
brilliance of their policies of open citizenship and manumission and had created a world in which Rome was perceived as the origin of misfortune, not its solution.

Of course, it can be argued that, using the tactics
that they did, the Romans were able to remain the great
power of the Western world for centuries; but again, they
achieved that preeminence *despite* their brutality, not because of it. All that Rome's penchant for destructive war
ensured was that its citizens lived with the constant threat
and demands of rebellion and conflict on their borders, as
well as a sense of insecurity that eventually bred a dangerous weariness with war inside the empire. That weariness,
in turn, contributed directly and substantially to a sense
of apathy toward national service generally and military
service in particular (to say nothing of an overall deca-
dence) that characterized later generations of Romans,
particularly young Romans. Had that apathy and aversion not arisen—had serving Rome not been often characterized by behavior with which enlightened, inventive
minds would not be identified—how much longer might
Rome have lasted, and how many of the most unsavory

aspects of Roman history might have been eliminated or at least redeemed? And above all, what would such a shift have meant for a world that was destined to be swallowed up by factional barbarism when Rome met its end?

That end came, for the western half of the empire, in the fifth century C.E., and it began, many assert, during one particularly cold winter when the Rhine froze over and offered German tribes an ice bridge into Roman territory. We have no truly reliable way of knowing whether any of those later tribesmen had been weaned, as had generations before them, on tales of Roman cruelty and the heroics of Arminius; but if such was indeed the case, the Romans had no one but themselves to blame.

The parallels to our own day are apparent, and they present us with a disturbing truth: when it comes to the problem, the practice, and the tactics of warfare against civilians, humanity has progressed very little over the last two thousand years.

CHAPTER TWO

DULCE BELLUM INEXPERTIS

Rome's two most important military legacies to the world, then, were the ideas that wars required no greater justification than the aggrandizement of power, and that there was no reason to treat noncombatants with any less severity than warriors. By thus confirming—even legitimizing—behavior that already characterized most non-Roman states and tribes, Rome placed these amoral traditions squarely at the center of nearly all international conflict that followed the breakup and collapse of the empire. Thus positioned, those traditions would prove remarkably impervious to the rise of a pair of global religions that claimed to be based on principles not only of morality but of compassion, mercy, and love—qualities difficult to reconcile with *any* violent activity, much less with the targeting of civilians as a method of spreading terror to undermine political cohesion and accrue wealth.

But as it happened, both Christianity and Islam, once they had graduated from the status of arcane cults, made little effort to change those unfortunate patterns of behavior. Indeed, as they assembled armies to forcibly spread their prophets' and their gods' messages, both religions discovered that Roman tactics could be made to serve their purposes admirably; and the work done by their legions of adherents was destined to achieve a level of savagery at which even the legions of Rome might well have balked.

For the first three centuries of its existence, Christianity emphasized its pacific (if not entirely pacifist) side; being for the most part an oppressed, although expanding, minority, its practitioners could do little else. But in 311, the eastern Roman emperor Galerius realized that if he was going to face the growing menace of enemies outside the empire, he needed to solidify the support of citizens within; and so he legitimized the Christian faith. Not long thereafter, the emperor Constantine, having emerged victorious from a long internal power struggle, consolidated his position by officially moving the capital of the empire east to Byzantium, away from the deteriorating situation in the west. Already for all practical purposes a Christian, Constantine assembled the first council of leaders of the various Christian sects within the empire at Nicaea; and when he decided to be baptized on his deathbed in 337, Constantine unknowingly signaled the onset of violence both inside the empire, where his three sons vied for power, and outside, where pagan tribes now had a new reason to resent and fear Rome.

Collapse in the west came a century later, and so great was the mayhem that ensued—and so focused was much of it on ordinary, noncombatant peasants and merchants—that the question of how to protect people who were vital to the day-to-day maintenance of civilized social order from assaults by roving bands of warriors became a pressing one. Upon hearing of the sack of Rome itself in 410 by Alaric, king of the Goths (much of whose army consisted, once again, of barbarian Roman-army veterans), the Christian bishop and philosopher Augustine of Hippo decided to write a treatise that would enumerate the alarming discrepancies between the "city of man" and the "city of God." His ruminations encompassed the conduct of international war and put forward one of the most imporant concepts in the history of military philosophy—that of the "just war."

It sounds almost ludicrous, today, that one of the era's great philosophers should actually feel it imperative to convince the world, even the Christian world, that in order to be legitimate war should be just. Yet we must remember the dominant military truth of human society to that point: wars *might* be "just" (generally by coincidence), but it was by no means *necessary* that they be just. For what exactly constituted just, when it came to war?

Was not an empire's or a nation's self-interest, or even the whim of a monarch (divine or otherwise), a just enough reason to fight? Perhaps it had been in the past, answered Augustine, but not anymore, given the state of violent anarchy into which much of the world had fallen. "The city of man," the philosopher lectured, "is a city of contention with opinions divided by foreign wars and domestic quarrels and by the demands for victories which either end in death or are merely momentary respites from further war. . . . Nevertheless it is wrong to deny that the aims of human civilization are good, for this is the highest end that man can achieve." "The purpose even of war is peace," he continued. "Even when men are plotting to disturb the peace, it is merely to fashion a new peace closer to the heart's desire." Finally, "when victory goes to the side that had a juster cause it is surely a matter for human rejoicing, and the peace is to be welcomed."

Thus the first requirement of just war is that it bring peace rather than perpetuate the cycle of plunder and rapine that benefits a few but destroys the lives of millions. As to specific rationalizations for fighting such wars, Augustine had but one: "A just war . . . is justified only by the injustice of an aggressor; and that injustice ought to be a source of grief to any good man, because it is human injustice." And what is injustice? It is anything that obstructs God's command that people live in "regulated fellowship"—that is, anything that resembled the unregulated, utterly chaotic division and bloodshed that Augustine saw rising in a great tide everywhere around him. Unfortunately, in 430 Augustine was to die, not within sight of any city of God on earth but as the barbarian Vandals were besieging his city of Hippo. But the intellectual seed that he had planted—the notion that wars should have just causes and that men should regulate their behavior in them, as much for practical (to preserve profitable, enjoyable peace) as for idealistic reasons—was to prove a hardy one and would germinate within the Christian world throughout the coming centuries of darkness in Europe.

But that idealistic seed had a sinister offshoot, too: for when Augustine spoke of restoring peace, he meant the peace of God. Violence undertaken in the name of the Christian faith, therefore, was also implicitly just; and one unintended result of his theories was a rationalization for holy war by Christians against unbelievers.

Meanwhile, during the centuries of European regression, the world's second most powerful international religion was developing on the Arabian peninsula. It, too, taught powerful lessons about how war should be conducted, as well as how civilians should be treated while it was being waged. The difficulty was (and remains) that, from the start of their movement in the seventh century, the prophet Muhammad and his followers found themselves in the position of needing to fight for their faith, as well as for territory in which to practice it and live. This sense of momentary expediency colors their sacred text, the Koran, with an often warlike tone—necessary at the time—that stands at singular variance with its equally earnest calls for compassion. For example, since Islam shared many prophets and holy traditions with Judaism and Christianity, members of those faiths were to receive mercy and tolerance from Muslims (where possible, that is); but as for pagans and polytheists, called "idolators" and "heathens," the order was simple: "Slay them wherever you find them." Yet the same chapter, or *surah,* of the holy book seemed at the same time to qualify this ruthlessness somewhat: "Fight for the sake of God those that fight against you," it read, "but do not attack them first. God does not love aggressors."

Many such passages of the Koran embodied two visions of war and two different attitudes toward faith and the enemies of Islam, and these discrepancies were destined to cause untold confusion and, for many non-Muslims, misery. "When you meet the unbelievers in the battlefield," says the forty-seventh *surah,* "strike off their heads and, when you have laid them low, bind your captives firmly. Then grant them their freedom or take a ransom from them, until war shall lay down her burdens." But again, in other passages one can quickly find the Prophet warning against unwarranted or excessive aggression: "Do not burn a plant, or cut a tree in the territory of

combatants." As the centuries of triumphant conversion
and political expansion wound on, however, it became increasingly difficult for Muhammad's inheritors to eluci-
date what was defense against aggression and what was
self-interested expansionism, particularly when their increasingly wealthy and powerful empire stretched from
Spain in the west to Asia Minor in the east. In a sense,
Muslims were facing their own crisis over what constituted a just war, and they desperately needed a clear,
easily accessible answer.

For like Christianity, Islam had not been born in a historical or cultural vacuum: it took root in areas and societies accustomed to long centuries of destructive war. The
tribal conflicts of Arabia, North Africa, and the Middle
East were no more enlightened or free of the practice of
terrorizing and plundering noncombatants than had been
those of the Roman empire (which had formally controlled many of those same territories). Therefore, whatever the compassionate exhortations of both Christianity
and Islam, they were from the beginning battling long-
standing military traditions that could not simply be
eradicated by good intentions. Even after Christianity
had become the official faith of the Roman empire, for
example, as well as of many of the barbarian tribes and
states bordering it, the unrestrained warlike tendencies of
that empire and those states and tribes showed few signs
of mitigation. And the tribal warfare that had always

characterized the lands that were incorporated into the Islamic empire simply evolved into consistent internecine feuding among various rival Muslim factions—Sunni, Shi'ite, Abbasid, Umayyad, Fatimid, and others—to say nothing of the periodic slaughtering of heathens. The habits of destructive war died hard—did not, in fact, die at all—and with the passage of time each world, Christian and Muslim, became so racked by the consequences of those habits that its leaders began to search hard for ways to, if not eradicate conflict, at least redirect it.

Unfortunately, both came up with the same solution.

By the tenth century the peoples of Europe—and more important the officials of the Christian church—had tried everything imaginable to induce the soldiers of their various kingdoms to give up their exploitative, randomly violent ways. They had even initiated the elaborate public-relations game known as chivalry, in tales of which knights were presented as noble, self-denying, respectful defenders of the weak and the helpless—a picture that could not have been more at odds with the truth. European peasants lived in a constant state of fear lest roving bands of knights and foot soldiers—even those in the service of their own dukes and kings—appear in their villages, sacking, raping, and killing until they were sated.

Finally, toward the end of the century, various church leaders in France, inspired by the thoughts of St. Augustine in *The City of God,* came up with the beginnings of an answer. Bishops began to propose to noblemen that they make virtue profitable by taxing and otherwise punishing their soldiers who brutalized peasants and other innocents. It was an unworkable idea—the soldiers were often more powerful than the nobles themselves—but the notion that certain people in society deserved to be free of the terrors of war and plundering eventually produced the much more momentous *Pax Dei* ("Peace of God") movement within the church. The *Pax Dei* soon evolved into the more specific *Treuga Dei* ("Truce of God") initiative, promulgated at Toulouges in 1027. By its terms war could be waged only Monday through Wednesday (all other days of the week being sacred to Christ) and never during Advent, Lent, and certain other feasts. The Council of Narbonne in 1054 further declared that no Christian should kill another Christian for any reason, "for whoever kills a Christian undoubtedly sheds the blood of Christ."

The church was proud of these initiatives, and hopeful of their efficacy, a hope shared by their peasant flocks; sadly, the nobles and knights of Europe—unwilling to share any more temporal power with the bishops than they had to—ignored the undertakings. They went on warring, raiding, and burning as before until finally church leaders realized that they had better look for other, less philosophically refined ways to vent the warriors' bloodthirstiness.

During this period, a different sort of evolution was taking place in the Muslim world, one of a characteristically dual nature. Despite the often violent nature of Muslim expansionism, the Islamic empire had by the early ninth century become the single greatest force for and preserver of intellectual vitality outside China: Muslim scholars, with a remarkable breadth of vision, were working hard to translate the scholarly works even of important infidels, while the caliph (the combined religious and secular leader of the Islamic world) al-Ma'mun was busy turning Baghdad into the intellectual and especially the scientific capital of the world. Islamic cities had made strides in sanitation and other public works—baths, lighting, gardens—that surpassed even Rome at its height. Yet factional violence between fellow Muslims, along with the persecution of heathens, never stopped: the context of Muhammad's early admonitions to spread the faith by the sword if necessary was forgotten, but the admonitions themselves became enshrined. Even during the caliphate of al-Ma'mun, a vicious fundamentalist movement opposed the cosmopolitanism of Baghdad. (Not surprisingly, the group became the spiritual inspiration for the Wahhabi sect in Saudi Arabia during the eighteenth century, which in turn sparked the twentieth-century fundamentalism of men such as Osama bin Laden.) There were periodic battles with the Byzantine (that is, the Eastern or Holy Roman) empire, troubles that grew over the next century. Then, in the middle of the eleventh century, one of the strongest Muslim communities—the Saljuq Turks—struck southward to try to take control of the fractious empire of the faithful.

Conquering Persia in the 1040s and Baghdad in 1055, the Saljuqs brought with them a seemingly insatiable thirst for war. They forcefully quelled the squabbling of factions in the eastern half of the Islamic empire, but Sunni Muslims held fast in Egypt, and war continued, focused on intervening Palestine. In fact, despite their accomplishments in the east, the arrival of the Turks spelled only heightened internal violence in much of the rest of the Islamic world, violence that many realized might be put to better use if it could be turned toward an external release. The Turks looked about for a suitable candidate on which to focus such outward aggression and soon found one in Palestine; but it was not their Sunni enemies.

For centuries, the Holy Roman Empire had held, and the rulers of the Muslim empire had respected, an unofficial protectorate over the Church of the Holy Sepulchre in Jerusalem (the purported tomb of Jesus), as well as over Christian pilgrims who journeyed to visit it. In the first decade of the eleventh century, the Fatimid caliph al-Hakim attempted to destroy the church; and some fifty years later the sultan of the Saljuqs, Alp Arslan, decided to formally end the qualification of Muslim supremacy im-

plied by the protectorate. The Byzantine emperor responded by attacking the sultan's forces, but he was
routed and captured at the Battle of Manzikert in 1071.
His successor in Constantinople cobbled together a defense of the remaining realm only after large areas of the
empire were overrun by the Saljuq army. It later became
clear that the Eastern Roman Empire had no choice but
to appeal to the western pope in Rome, Urban II, for
help.

It so happened that Urban II, who had inherited the
problem of a set of European nobles who cared nothing
for the Truce of God movement, desperately needed just
such an appeal and just such a cause. In 1095, almost
with a sigh of relief, he called for warriors to fight the
Muslim menace, saying of the European knights: "Let
those who have long been robbers now be soldiers of
Christ. Let those who once fought against brothers and
relatives now rightfully fight against barbarians."

The call went out, among Muslims and Christians
alike, for a defense of the faith, one that, ironically, was
inspired in both cases by the need to get faithful warriors to stop victimizing noncombatants in their own
communities—hardly the last time that international war
would be used as a way to solve internal problems. Yet the
ensuing conflict would be no quick fix; rather, it evolved
into a series of wars in which the victimization of those
same noncombatants reached extremes never imagined

by those who began it all. This presents us with another enduring truth about the tactics of terror: they must never be viewed as an expedient or a controllable instrument of policy, one which, after its purpose has been served, will simply burn itself out. For the fire of terrorism is a self-sustaining one and once ignited must be either starved or forcibly extinguished.

There exists no greater proof of this lesson than the wars that came to be called the Crusades, which instilled so powerful a desire for revenge and retaliatory violence among both Muslims and Christians that we continue to see and feel its effects today. (When, after the September 11, 2001, attack on the United States, American president George W. Bush thoughtlessly announced the need for a "crusade" against terror, the word set off alarm bells throughout the Islamic world, and he had to work hard to undo the offense.) The question of who was to blame for the centuries of bitterly destructive war is almost moot. Certainly the Christians would have been better off seeking a diplomatic solution to the problem of the Jerusalem protectorate; but then the protectorate was not the real reason that thousands of European nobles and their men-at-arms invaded the Muslim empire. As for the forces of Islam, their passionate declarations to the faithful that the infidels must be repulsed and destroyed often masked—as they had since the early days of their empire—self-serving expansionism and a desire to annex new cities and lands, as well as to force greater loyalty and obedience out of their own subjects. This is not to say that some good and devout men did not serve on both sides during the Crusades; it is simply to contend that such men were likely unaware of the machinations of their leaders. And if they were leaders themselves (as in the case, most notably, of the fabled Muslim warrior-statesman Salah-al-din), they used their dramatic battle-field feats to consolidate their own domestic power.

And they did so with uniform ruthlessness toward not only warriors but noncombatants. Reports became routine of the complete extermination of entire cities by both Christians and Muslims (for when the Christian warriors established a foothold in the holy land, their civilian followers peopled it); and the details of these reports involve forms of death and torture that almost defy even our seasoned contemporary imaginations. The intention on both sides was, as usual, to so terrify and impress the enemy that he would abandon his allegiance to his leader and his cause. Its results were equally familiar—and counterproductive. The murderous righteousness of the Christian invaders inspired not submission on the part of the Muslims but all the retaliatory fury of a faith born and bred in armed conflict; and that fury only intensified the Westerners' determination to stay and exact their own vengeance. Thus neither side could claim victory when the Crusades finally came to an end. True, the

Muslims could say that they had driven the invaders back out, a result that—since the Christian invaders had been the first to resort during the Crusades to the widespread extermination of enemy civilians—was to be expected. But vengeful Islam had no more improved its position in the world than had Christianity. Worse yet, the Crusades did not bring unity or peace to either the Christian or the Islamic portions of the globe. In fact, they only hastened the process of fragmentation in both.

In short, if the tactics of terror employed during the Crusades taught one lesson overall it was that institutionalized religion offered the average citizen no hope whatsoever of escape from the agonies of destructive war. This notion contributed substantially to the eventual dissipation—one can hardly say resolution—of the long series of conflicts. And while the Muslim world admonished its members to show more diligent faith through participation in further expansion under their new and more blatantly mercenary Turkish leaders (expansion that would in fact do little to prevent still more factional violence within the Islamic community), in the West the failure of the church to resolve, among other things, the issues of what constituted a just war and who should be protected from its effects led many citizens to look again to princes rather than priests for protection. In this trend can be found some of the early roots of the next great Western political trend: nationalism.

It can thus be accurately said that while the butchery of the Crusades produced no clear victor, it did produce a definite loser: the Catholic Church. In keeping with the idea that those who unleash terror ultimately undermine their own cause most of all, we can observe, in the generations following the last of the Crusades, a marked erosion of the spiritual and worldly authority of the church in the realms of politics and war. Less and less did the peoples of Europe turn to priests for answers concerning international disputes and how they should be conducted. Secular authorities began to fill the role, just as secular leaders began to assert their independent political authority and repudiate the need to be approved by Rome. This trend would ultimately take hold during the Reformation and would finally result in the great age of divine monarchs, whose legitimacy was granted (they claimed) directly by God, not by the pope.

Thus, while wise and pious men such as Thomas Aquinas spent much of the thirteenth century revisiting the issues of when and how good Christians should make war (without, in Aquinas's case, reaching any particularly impressive conclusions), by the middle of the fourteenth century the tendency among citizens to rely on sovereigns for more practical protection became so widespread that a seemingly minor territorial and dynastic dispute between France and England drew enough supporters and participants to generate a war that lasted for the absurdly disproportionate span of a century. And during that Hundred Years War truly ominous new developments in attitudes toward and practices of warfare against civilians took place, developments that would dramatically worsen the lot of a broad range of noncombatants.

For as it turned out, the ancillary military role of a civilian in a clearly defined *nation* was far less ambiguous than it had been in the days when states were geographically unstable or, as in the case of the Holy Roman Empire, ever changing in their ethnic makeup and dynasties. The rise of nationalism brought general agreement among rulers and warriors that *every* inhabitant of a country, by assenting to citizenship, was in some way a part of that nation's war machine. The rural peasant that the church had always held up as the supreme example of the pastoral noncombatant, for instance, was now viewed as one of the prime supporters of a given war effort; for without his grain and his tax revenue, no king or prince could feed his army's horses or pay his soldiers. Indeed, the church itself paid taxes to secular princes, and so church lands and church wealth became fair game, and priests and nuns found themselves the targets of armed robbery and violation with increasing frequency. All the terrorizing tactics that had been practiced before the Crusades were intensified, but with a terrible twist: there was an unnerving new shamelessness among the combatants, who had come to understand that depredations against civilians were now central to all military campaigns.

There was very little opposition to this thinking, and not much of the little had any effect. But that which did initially came, remarkably enough, not from clerical philosophers or even national monarchs but from a few insightful military commanders. These few were able to see that warfare waged so systematically and harshly against civilians might well inspire such deep hostility among the inhabitants of cities and the countryside that the conqueror's task of future administration would be made extremely difficult, and perhaps even impossible in cases of extreme brutality.

This highly unusual perspective was perhaps best explained by Sir John Fastolf, an adviser to the English king in 1435. The Hundred Years War was at that moment taking a decided turn in France's favor, and it was Fastolf's opinion that the fault lay with the English policy of engaging in lengthy, brutal sieges of French castles. Fastolf objected to such sieges not simply because they were costly and ineffectual but also because of the extreme hatred that was being bred by the tactic of starvation and bombardment with cannon. Fastolf advised the king to abandon such methods and to break his forces into more limited contingents. These should move rapidly through the French countryside, "brennyng and distruynge alle the lande as thei pas, bothe hous, corne, veignes, and alle treis that beren fruyte for mannys suste-naunce, and alle bestaile that may not be driven, to be de-stroiede." There was little that was revolutionary about this much of Fastolf's ideas; it was his next recommenda-tion that was unprecedented for a military man. Actual combat, he declared, should occur only "betwixt men of werre and men of werre"—an idea that had previously been voiced primarily by idealistic clergymen and in chivalric fantasies. But Fastolf's advocacy of a distinction between civilian property that might have military value and the civilians themselves was empirical: having spent years in the field, he claimed that the French policy of at-tacking the populace indiscriminately was "cruelle and sharpe, without sparing of any parsone."

The implication was clear, and in the wake of the fool-ish and wasteful Hundred Years War it gained adherence not only among military minds but among legal scholars as well. If the excesses of war were to be mitigated, it was not going to be through appeals to religion or morality made by priests; soldiers themselves would have to devise ways of controlling the excesses of their men, in an effort to stop the erosion of civilian loyalty. At the same time, jurists and lawyers would have to hammer out rules for behavior among nations, rules that would take the place of discarded clerical edicts and movements.

The concept was far more momentous than it seemed

to almost anyone at the time: at last select members of a class of men who could actually influence the wartime situation in the field—military commanders—had begun to see that tactics of terror, while they might gratify the angry, vengeful imperatives of their rulers, their soldiers, and many wronged citizens, were detrimental to their own nations' causes. At the same time, the age-old perspective on the problem provided by religious philosophers such as St. Augustine was stood on its head by experts in secular law, who introduced the idea that even though the law of God could do little to affect the horrors of conflict, the law of man might do better by coming up with specific, binding international codes.

For the next four hundred years, it was among the ranks of military officers and experts in international law that the debate over warfare against civilians was most meaningfully waged, between those who saw the tactic as simply inevitable and those who opposed it out of enlightened self-interest. As for the church, more and more of its officials simply fell into despair on the subject of armed conflict. Worse still, when the wars of the Reformation began, some even joined the ranks of those who considered civilians legitimate targets of destructive operations—thereby squandering what little authority the church had left to speak on such matters.

Meanwhile, those Christian humanist philosophers who had tried so hard to establish rules of war that would be acceptable to God and Nature also abandoned the effort before long. In 1511, even before Martin Luther nailed his theses to a church door in Saxony, Erasmus of Rotterdam prefigured their attitude by bitterly writing of society in general and bellicose, exploitative clergymen in particular, "Moreover, since the Christian church was founded on blood, strengthened by blood, and increased in blood, they continue to manage its affairs by the sword as if Christ has perished and can no longer protect his own people in his own way. War is something so monstrous that it befits wild beasts rather than men, so crazy that the poets even imagine that it is let loose by the Furies, so deadly that it sweeps like a plague through the world, so unjust that it is best carried on by the worst type of bandit, so impious that it is quite alien to Christ." In another, less loquacious mood, Erasmus would declare simply, *"Dulce bellum inexpertis"*: "War is sweet to those who know nothing of it." And with that the debate was handed to a new generation of philosophers, men who had less interest in what pleased Christ than in how violent affairs between powerful states might be rationally managed.

CHAPTER THREE

INDUSTRY AND CUNNING

In many contemporary studies and treatments of terrorism—from serious scholarly works to film and television dramas that merely pretend to seriousness—it has been asserted that our current problem is historically rooted in the beliefs and behavior of several violently mystical groups, some dating back as far as the Middle Ages. In the case of Islamic fundamentalist terrorism, for instance, the suggested historical precedent has often been a group of medieval Shi'ite Muslims who first split off as part of a sect known as Isma'ilis and then further splintered into a peculiar but deadly group known as the *hashshashin* cult. This shadowy organization used (as the name implies) hashish as a means of first reaching a state of religious ecstasy and then girding themselves for their sacred work: the murder of both Christians and

Muslims they considered enemies of their faith and their sect. (The English word *assassin* is derived from *hashshashin*.)

But tracing the roots of terrorism back to such fringe groups, deadly as they may have been, is both misleading and dangerous. Born out of the indignant (and in many ways understandable) refusal to accord terrorists the status of actual soldiers, such categorization only serves to mislead the public as to the nature and extent of the threat we now face: for terrorism's real roots are no more exotic or mystical than they are obscure. Terrorism is the expression of a constant theme in military history—the deliberate targeting of civilians in order to undermine their support for the policies of their political leaders—whereas the purposes of medieval cults of violence were never so coherent. The goal of the Assassins, for example, was not to influence civilian political views but to actually kill political and religious leaders; and their murders were rarely if ever followed up by any organized attempt to seize power. However resistant we may be to the idea, what we now know as international terrorism is part of a military tradition, albeit a savagely violent one; and as we proceed into an examination of how that tradition survived into the early modern period, it is important to bear in mind that the men responsible for that survival were not fringe lunatics or mystics. They were soldiers and statesmen, many of them well respected, who generally did their work not in the shadowy corners of the world but in the halls of national power—just as today's terrorists could not survive if they did not enjoy the protection, funding, and support of sovereign states.

By recognizing terrorism as part of a military tradition, we need neither ennoble its agents nor offer them the same rights that uniformed combatants enjoy under the various Geneva protocols. But the first rule of battling any enemy, even one whose methods we despise, is to know him and, if not respect him, at least respect the nature and scope of the danger he poses. Treating the modern terrorist as anything other than a distinct type of soldier only gives him more power by keeping his behavior outside the realm of accurate understanding.

One of the most crucial pieces of that understanding is an appreciation of how the practice of destructive war was kept alive from the medieval era, which few people have trouble accepting as a brutal and uncivilized time, into the early modern period, when institutions of government, military organization, and civil society attained forms that we can recognize as the forerunners of our own. The sad truth is that this transition took place with remarkable ease. Indeed, when we look at warfare in the late fifteenth and early sixteenth centuries, with its continued general acceptance of the butchering of noncombatants as a calculated psychological and political tool, the only truly unprecedented and surprising fact is that a

handful of soldiers and jurists somehow found the where-
withal to try to change things.

They were given an opportunity, at least in part, because of the significant democratization of international
conflict that came about as a result of the era's technological advances, particularly in the design and production of firearms. The mounted warrior, once the scourge
of the countryside and ruler of the battlefield, had already
seen his supremacy challenged by the development of,
among other weapons, the longbow, which had enabled
such crucial victories as that of the English at Agincourt
in 1415. Soon thereafter, the presence of crude cannon
began to expedite the conduct of siege warfare. But by the
end of the century both cannon and handheld firearms
had been greatly improved and made accessible not only
to rulers and knights but to the individual citizens that
made up political and religious factions. Traditional rules
governing the conduct of war were suddenly being rewrit-
ten by people who would once have been thought un-
worthy to even attempt the practice of arms—people
upon whom, as is the case with terrorists in our own day,
much of the world was horrified to bestow the status of
soldiers.

In other words, war was suddenly and clearly exposed
as not a chivalric contest of noble worthies in God's service but a generally unromantic instrument of political
policy. Clearly, new arrangements needed to be made if

heads of state were to integrate these sundry developments into the conduct of international relations.

The first rulers to recognize this situation were Italian. Several insightful princes on that peninsula, along with their military advisers, came up with a deceptively simple solution to the dilemma: a new type of war, they decided, required a new type of soldier. But whole armies and populations could hardly be trained in these new methods quickly enough to grapple with the new wave of violence being bred by the ongoing erosion of the authority of the Catholic Church. Shrewdly recognizing this gap and stepping in to fill it came groups of *condottieri*—mercenary captains—who began to raise independent armies of professional soldiers who contracted themselves out to warring rulers. The practice immediately became so successful and widespread that individual *condottieri* bands sometimes found themselves fighting on both sides of a given conflict within the same year; yet the most remarkable thing about these men was not their avarice but their philosophy of war.

Professional mercenary armies naturally had very little interest in the high casualty rates that had characterized medieval warfare: beyond being unfortunate, such bloody tactics were expensive. In addition, the new advances in artillery design meant that sieges could be prosecuted in far less time, as castle walls that had been designed to withstand catapult and trebuchet missiles were no match for quality cannon. Finally, infantrymen bearing even rudimentary firearms could gain the advantage in the field much more quickly than could men armed with swords or even longbows. The real problem for the *condottieri*, then, was not to find new and better ways to kill but rather to devise methods of harnessing the decisive potential of their troops and weapons with the least possible bloodshed. As two noted *condottieri*, Paolo Vitelli and Prospero Colonna, themselves explained, "wars are won rather by industry and cunning than by the actual clash of arms."

This germ of modern progressive warfare appalled many observers at the time. Promulgated by mercenaries, it seemed to lack not only any sense of patriotism but also the chivalric martial virtues that had already been popularized in such *chansons de geste* as *The Song of Roland* and that were still being celebrated in epics like Thomas Malory's *Le Morte d'Arthur.* In addition, Italians of the age were preoccupied with a similarly romanticized conception of the battlefield doings of the legions of ancient Rome. (Although the *condottieri* admired many of the strategic concepts developed by men such as Julius Caesar, the *condottieri* wars had none of the scope or bloodshed of Roman campaigns.) Even the usually incisive Niccolò Machiavelli had fallen prey to the nostalgia for the cataclysmic violence of ancient Rome, and he decried the new form of *condottieri* conflict, complaining that in one half-day encounter "nobody was killed; only some horses were wounded and a few prisoners made on either side." Such observers were utterly blind to the point of the *condottieri*'s strategy and tactics, which was, as one expert on the period, Sir Charles Oman, put it, "to manoeuvre the enemy into an impossible situation, and then capture him, rather than exhaust him by a series of costly battles." Once captured, such enemies could be ransomed for healthy sums; but the larger point was that war was now being conceived of as something in which victory rather than destruction was the object, as well as something to be conducted by professionals against professionals. Civilians were not to be deliberately involved; indeed, they were almost irrelevant.

The *condottieri*'s moment, however, was brief indeed. By the early sixteenth century, Italy, like the rest of Europe, found itself preoccupied with the wars of the Reformation, during which the bloodlust of the Middle Ages was not only revived but intensified by the new weapons that were readily available to all parties. Like the American Civil War and the First World War, the wars of the Reformation were particularly savage because of a deadly mixture of outdated military thinking and progressive military technology. During the first half of the century, the conflicts were for the most part civil wars, with Protestants and Catholics vying for control of individual principalities, but in the second half larger lines had been drawn. Spain emerged as the great Catholic power, with England as its northern counterweight and such countries as France and the Netherlands shifting from one side of the scales to the other as Catholic and Protestant rulers and factions alternately seized and lost control. As in the Crusades, religious fervor rationalized the most barbaric actions: any civilian who practiced any form of either Catholicism or Protestantism was seen as involved in the conflict and was therefore treated as a legitimate target.

Once again, it was the Catholic Church (along with Catholic rulers, whose allegiance to Rome underwent a sudden reinvigoration at the prospect of new political and territorial gains) that reached most quickly for the weapons of terror. Not only were Protestant communities ravaged and their inhabitants slaughtered but the Inquisition was allowed—even encouraged—to degenerate from an already fearsome instrument of purification into an organ of widespread persecution and torture. Many Protestant leaders and armies swiftly answered this brutality in kind, but once again it was the Catholic Church's interests that would ultimately suffer the most. The early modern period was to see the steady erosion not only of Rome's power but of that of the Catholic empires as well, along with a complementary strengthening of their Protestant rivals, Britain and, eventually, the Netherlands.

The signal moment in this shift in the balance of European power was triggered, if not fully caused, by events far from Europe. Spain's rise to preeminence in the first half of the sixteenth century was funded to a large extent by the gold and silver it steadily extracted from the New World after the conquest and genocidal decimation of that region's most powerful native empires, the Aztecs and Incas, by the ruthless yet celebrated adventurers Hernando Cortés and Francisco Pizarro. As Spain's power and arrogance grew during the second half of the century, privateers (mercenary naval raiders) began to raid Spanish commerce with the New World; and it was the efforts of those privateers in the pay of England—firmly ruled by a Protestant monarch, Queen Elizabeth I—that did the most damage. Initially hijacking Spanish shipments of slaves from Africa to the Americas, the English raiders—most notably Sir Francis Drake—soon realized that attacks on the burgeoning treasure ships of His Catholic Majesty, King Philip II of Spain, were far more popular at home (the slave trade never having enjoyed universal support in England), far more lucrative, and (perhaps of greatest importance to the impertinent Drake), far more annoying to King Philip. And so the "sea dogs," as they were affectionately known in England, expanded their quest for Spanish gold and silver, with Queen Elizabeth's generally covert backing. Before long, they also expanded their operations to include those Spanish ports throughout the Americas that served as transfer depots for precious metals.

Such behavior unquestionably constituted piracy, a practice that had distinct similarities to modern-day terrorism. But there was a wrinkle in the British version of privateering that was both unique and critical, one that is particularly exemplified in the person of Drake. As the noted historian of piracy David Cordingly has written, "Ambitious and piratical by nature, [Drake] plundered and looted every Spanish vessel he could lay his hands on and made himself a rich man. He was bold and decisive in action, and yet displayed a remarkable sensitivity in his dealings with his men, who adored him, and with captured enemies, who regarded him with admiration." A man of humble origins and, so far as the court of King Philip was concerned, distinctly *un*soldierly manners and practices, Drake had a pronounced sympathy for the average citizen entangled in the violent web of war, and he made every practical effort to ensure that his men's plundering was confined to goods and structures directly connected to the Spanish government's economic machinery. In so doing, he further advanced the notion that military action—even military action not officially sanctioned by any government—did not have to depend on the abuse and wholesale elimination of civilians for success, as well as the idea that the nation which avoided such tactics could realistically expect to see its domestic solidarity rise in unison with its international prestige.

Never was this idea more clearly demonstrated than

in 1588, when an enraged King Philip dispatched his
mighty armada to the English Channel, only to suffer a
humiliating defeat at the hands of Queen Elizabeth's
smaller fleet but superior commanders—particularly
Drake, who had by now become Philip's most despised
nemesis. Few historical moments have so deserved the
label of turning point. True, European religious conflict
went on for another sixty years, through the astoundingly
barbaric Thirty Years War, during which slaughters of entire civilian communities were commonplace. But that
conflict can be quite plausibly seen as the death throes of
the particular religious insanity that had plagued Europe
since the Crusades and that was now being killed off
by secular power politics. The effective last stand of any
great power that could genuinely call itself Catholic was
made in 1588: after that, both Spain and the Holy
Roman Empire entered into long, incremental, but irre-
versible processes of fatal decline, while the greatness of
"Catholic" France would be revived only when her statesmen (even those drawn, like the powerful Cardinal
Richelieu, from the clergy) learned to concern themselves
with worldly force rather than religion.

As for England, it had begun the process of becoming
a modern empire, one that would outstrip in size and
power not only its former Catholic rivals but their old
Muslim enemies as well. This remarkable achievement
was due in no small part to the willingness of English

leaders to initiate a long process of more equitable treatment of their citizens at home and then export those dramatic advances in constitutional government abroad as their colonies multiplied. Then, too, the invention of new industrial technologies, new weapons, and new military strategies and tactics did not hinder the empire's growth: industry and cunning would find an unrivaled home in what would eventually become Great Britain, a fact that would lift the empire's catalog of achievements—politically, militarily, and even morally—far above those of its predecessors.

Of course, Britain's record of living up to those ideals overseas was not perfectly consistent. Indeed, in some cases British behavior failed so completely to match the high moral standards they had set for themselves that they were confronted with violent opposition, which they attempted to repress with some of the most infamous methods of destructive war the world had yet known. This was to give rise to whole new breeds of combatants that the civilized citizens of London, forgetting such precedents as the piratical exploits of their own Sir Francis Drake, could not bear to call *real* soldiers.

CHAPTER FOUR

COVENANTS WITHOUT THE SWORD

By the terms of the Treaty of Westphalia, which ended the Thirty Years War in 1648, various European provinces changed hands, drastically altering the hierarchy of continental power. In addition, Protestantism became an established fact of European life, and the Swiss republic became a state: for such a broad range of results some eight million or more people, most of them noncombatants, lost their lives. Many voices condemned this vaguely organized lunacy after its conclusion, but the most eloquent critic, and in many ways the most important one, had delivered his assessment when the war was not yet half over. "I saw prevailing throughout the Christian world a license in making war," wrote the Dutch jurist Huigh de Groot (who became known as Grotius) in 1625, "of which even barbarous nations should be ashamed; resorting to arms for trivial or for no reasons at all, and when arms were taken up no reverence left for human or divine law, exactly as if a single edict had released a madness driving men to all kinds of crime." The statement was part of Grotius's introduction to *The Rights of War and Peace,* an earnest and learned effort to discover some sort of natural law of nations that might serve to guard against and mitigate such barbarities as Grotius was himself observing.

Noble as the effort may have been, it was as doomed to failure as every similar undertaking since St. Augustine's had been. Indeed, in attempting to determine what constituted a just war Grotius reached conclusions that had their roots in Augustine's: according to natural law, he wrote, human beings and states have first and foremost the right to defend themselves. And, tangentially, just as a society of human beings has the right to punish a member who has committed a crime against another, so a nation or a group of nations have the right to punish a state or ruler that has injured another unjustly. But even in a just war, Grotius went on, the aggrieved party must conduct itself within the bounds of what is—again, according to natural law—humane and responsible; the rules of civil society do not disappear simply because countries decide to go to war. Indeed, those rules are all the more incumbent on the participants at such times, in order to prevent war from degenerating into mayhem. With this in mind, Grotius declared that not only noncombatants but prisoners of war must be treated decently; that civil-ian property must be respected, as must the status of neu-tral parties; that treaties must be honored over time, not used as temporary, self-serving tactics; and, again, that nations must wage only just war.

Other jurists soon followed Grotius's example by enu-merating what they believed were essential regulations for this new interpretation of "international law." Commen-tators such as Samuel Pufendorf recommended every-thing from European congresses to a European union as methods of enforcement, yet the ongoing horrors of war on the Continent made a mockery of all their efforts. The dilemma was as apparent then as it remains today: the citizens of individual nations obey laws because there is a commonly recognized authority that will act against them if they do not. But to what conceivable interna-tional authority would a nation submit for censure if told that it had committed a crime against another? And even if a diplomatic or legal body could be established to pass such censures, what military force would carry out the punishment? Such measures were destined to be tough practical propositions in the twentieth century; they proved almost laughable in the seventeenth. The ink on the Treaty of Westphalia was scarcely dry before Euro-peans were back at the business of slaughtering one another's civilians wholesale, in the ongoing effort to influence the behavior of the kings and princes to whom the safety of those noncombatants had, at least nominally, been entrusted.

Yet if Grotius and his colleagues failed in the short term, they did at least succeed in pointing out that the level of violence in Europe had grown past destructive: it was becoming suicidal. The cycle of massacre and reprisal had such widespread effects that daily life—and, even more important to those in power, daily commerce—was becoming an impractical proposition. Though the idea of creating institutions of international law did not immediately catch on, it did reinforce the argument that conflict needed reforming and regulating. The first demonstration of a workable program for such reform and regulation came as a result not of an international conflict, however, but of a civil one; and once again the venue for such progress was England.

During the civil war that would eventually see an ascendant English Parliament try its politically obtuse yet arrogant king on charges of treason and tyranny and sentence him to be beheaded, several military officers in the parliamentary army grew determined to limit the impact of the conflict on English noncombatants, as well as to improve the performance of their men in the field. These goals were correctly seen as interrelated, and both were eventually achieved, not through philosophical or legalistic exhortations but through drastically increased military training and discipline. Not surprisingly, the most important of the officers behind this movement were Puritans: and the ablest of them, Oliver Cromwell, found in his "New Model Army" the instrument with which not only to win the civil war but to ensure that Parliament, when it took over the reins of power from the monarchy and immediately began to abuse the people almost as badly as had the executed Charles I, could be forcibly dissolved. Cromwell then became England's first and only military dictator, an event as momentous for the world as it was for his own nation. In a very limited time—and using policies that were, while admittedly restrictive, not nearly as unpopular as subsequent generations of royalists and historians depicted them—Cromwell restored first domestic stability and then the international might and prestige of England, all of which had suffered badly under Charles and during the civil war. By the time the Lord Protector (as Cromwell was officially styled) died in 1658, England needed fear no other European power, and its colonial expansion was proceeding at a pace to match or exceed its continental rivals.

All this had been made possible by a single, seemingly unportentous core policy: effective military discipline. Soldiers were drilled hard by stern officers; punished severely for infractions; and forced to wear uniforms, for one of the chief problems of sixteenth- and seventeenth-century conflict had been that combatants and noncombatants generally looked much alike, which often led to meaningless casualties during engagements, while making it easier for troops to desert. The results of these seemingly mundane reforms went beyond anything the religious humanists or the jurists had been able to achieve with their eloquent, elaborate calls for the protection of civilians, and in this fact there was a simple, concrete lesson to be learned. Indeed, it is one that still holds true today, though it is still ignored with remarkable frequency: strict discipline of soldiers, especially regarding their interactions with civilians, can foster general social stability to such an extent that the political loyalties of those same citizens may well change in order that they may be allowed to benefit from that stability. In other words, ironically, the alteration of political loyalties sought by those who terrorize civilians is actually most quickly and effectively achieved by refraining from those same tactics.

That Cromwell was able to absorb this lesson so thoroughly was the key to his success in England; that he forgot it, however, was to be the cause of his demonization in Ireland. During the English civil war, fleeing royalist officers, aristocrats, and soldiers sought sanctuary on that neighboring island, and Cromwell pursued them there. Then, following the pattern established by otherwise enlightened English rulers since Henry II in the twelfth century, Cromwell violated all of the precepts that had rewarded him so well at home: he not only brutally punished the royalists but did the same to their Irish sympathizers, along with many civilians who had no interest in the war at all. The latter groups were forcibly relocated into designated zones in the western half of the island, and their lands were offered to Parliamentary veterans. Cromwell's defenders have maintained that this uncharacteristic behavior was retribution for Irish massacres of British soldiers and settlers years earlier. But even if this is true, the temporary but apparent inability to comprehend that terror must never be answered in kind is a notable and puzzling blind spot in Cromwell's otherwise expansive vision. His excesses fed the growing cycle of outrage and counteroutrage that was destined to grow into the nightmare of modern Irish terrorism—of which we shall hear more.

The lessons taught by Cromwell's experiences in England were, as noted, the result of a civil, rather than an international, conflict; and he promulgated them through methods most readily available to a dictator. Yet military dictatorship, or tyranny of any other kind, has never been in and of itself a guarantee of administrative success: history is littered with failed tyrants who did nothing for the lot of their own people—indeed, Charles I was one of them. And since civil wars are traditionally *more* bitter than international conflicts, not less, there seemed no reason why the lessons offered by Cromwell's experience could not be applied to the ongoing violence afflicting the Continent. But the vanity, viciousness, and obstinacy of Europe's rulers continued to make them utterly insensitive to the suffering of either their own or their enemies' citizens, as well as to the ominous political implications of that suffering. True, a drift toward hiring and maintaining standing armies of native professionals and foreign mercenaries, commanded by generals of at least some competence did begin during the Thirty Years War; and this might have proved an ameliorating trend, for it brought with it signs of the kind of professionalism and discipline that had worked so well in England. But in general, the changes and improvements were unsystematic— or even, in some cases, unintentional.

No example better demonstrates the enduring belief of various European rulers in the political power of destructive war than that of France under Louis XIV. Prior to the renowned monarch's ascension in 1643, France had, under the guidance of that supreme hypocrite and master of pliable morality Cardinal Richelieu, already adopted the diplomatic policy (if such it could be called) of *raison d'état,* or "reason of state." Any alliance, any war, any move in the brutal continental political game, however morally repugnant, had been deemed permissible so long as it served France's interests. When Louis took the throne, he seemed initially to offer a respite from the cynicism that had kept France (and indeed the rest of Europe, since every other power had quickly adopted *raison d'état* as its guiding diplomatic principle) perpetually enmeshed in war. But Louis ultimately proved just as brutal and even more cunning than Richelieu. For while the cardinal had never succeeded in completely concealing his true nature with clerical vestments, Louis draped his own ruthlessness much more effectively in the ornate and highly popular robes and persona of "the Sun King." Excited and duped by Louis's exhortations, whole generations of Frenchmen were swallowed up by his plans to frustrate France's rivals and make himself the superpower of Europe.

Acting with such dubious tact that he inspired nearly every other power in Europe to ally against him, Louis did manage to bludgeon his way to securing defensible borders and a preeminent position of power for his nation, which had not enjoyed entirely favorable fortunes of war during the previous century. But such a king as Louis was not to be satisfied with so temperate an achievement as security. He began to look past the borders of France, with the intent of crippling his enemies. His method for achieving this goal included a specific and personal contribution to warfare against civilians, one that came in the form of creating—or trying to create—a cordon sanitaire (one of the most repugnant of the many euphemisms that the tactics of terror have enjoyed throughout history) on each of France's frontiers.

In the Rhineland, in Catalonia, and in Piedmont, French troops burned farms, killed and raped civilians, destroyed cultivated fields and livestock, and stole what little remained in order to create a wide swath of land around France that would be a dead zone to hostile armies. The official rationalization for this effort rested on the same sort of petty territorial and dynastic grievances that had troubled Europe for years; and they produced not one but two major conflicts that further resembled those earlier encounters in their brutality, their considerable length, and finally in the fact that the nation that had exhibited the most consequential and determined willingness to campaign against noncombatants—France—lost the primacy its king had schemed so hard to achieve. The rulers and citizens of the countries ravaged by Louis's troops were only steeled by the severity of the French: in the end, Louis was humiliated at the Battle of Blenheim in 1704 and had to salvage what he could through diplomacy, rendering most if not all the destruction caused by his reign meaningless.

The rest of the world, in the meantime, was experiencing the proliferation of still more types of destructive war, some of which started in Europe and were exported by colonists and the garrisons that protected them, while others represented the traditional warring styles of indigenous populations. Most prevalent among the latter were the ongoing conquests by, and internecine wars be-

tween, the major factions—Mameluke, Ottoman, and
Mughal—that had come to dominate the Muslim world
in the wake of the devastation wrought by the Mongol invasion of the Islamic empire in the thirteenth century.

The Mongols themselves would seem to deserve some
mention in any history of warfare against civilians, for
surely there have been few peoples less capable of dis-
criminating between warriors and noncombatants during
military action and more given to enthusiastically harsh
treatment of both varieties. But, as had earlier been the
case with another marauding people, the Huns, one fact
about the Mongols predominates in this context: terror
was not a policy for them—it was simply a way of life.
When Mongol warriors descended on their noncombatant victims, it was not with the intention of influencing
those victims' loyalty to their leaders; it was simply to indulge their own passion for rapine. The Mongols are fas-
cinating and historically significant on a number of levels;
but their importance to this area of military and political
history is virtually nil.

Nor did the Mongol invasion of the Muslim empire
initially indicate that they would have any importance to
cultural pursuits in that part of the world, being as they
sacked such great Islamic intellectual centers as Baghdad.
But the Mongols became Muslims themselves soon thereafter and quickly began to interbreed with the Turks, at
which point their importance increased dramatically. For

the progeny of this interbreeding would assume responsibility for the conduct of what remained, even in its fractious and somewhat reduced state, one of the great empires of the world. But while the Turco-mongol tribes did eventually learn to appreciate the great intellectual and artistic achievements of their Arab predecessors, they also found that the admonitions to violent evangelism contained in the Koran fit nicely with their native inclination toward rapacious, nomadic conquest. The marriage of these two traditions (Islamic evangelism and Turco-mongol plundering) soon produced striking revisions of the maps of three continents—as well as savagely inventive new forms of destructive war.

By the end of the fifteenth century, the Ottoman Turks had heralded their rise to Muslim preeminence by sweeping northwest to the frontiers of Bulgaria and Hungary. Along the way, they captured and sacked Constantinople, largely through the use of bronze cannon that were far more advanced than anything that could be found in Europe at the time. Simultaneously, they subdued their Mameluke cousins in Egypt and Palestine, so that by the mid-sixteenth century the Ottoman empire stretched from central Europe to North Africa—all this from what had once been a tribe of tough nomadic herdsmen who had originally been hired by the Arabs and the Saljuq Turks in the thirteenth century to fight against the Mongol invaders. (The Arabs and Seljuks had thereby committed the mistake of believing that one can use and then dispense with agents of violent mayhem, just as the Romans had done with their own barbarian subjects.) To the east of the Ottomans, those other great inheritors of the khans, the Mughal (an Arabic derivation of *Mongol*) Turks, had long since pushed beyond the fourteenth-century empire of the infamous Tamerlane in and around Persia to take control first of Afghanistan and its capital, Kabul, and then of the wondrous set of principalities, Hindu and otherwise, that lay to the southeast: India.

It has become the lot of art historians to rationalize the violence and oppression of the Ottoman and Mughal Turks by citing the cultural heights to which both empires eventually rose; and indeed, those artistic and intellectual achievements cannot be denied. But it does our understanding of the nature and history of warfare against civilians no more good to whitewash the way in which these achievements were facilitated than it does to explain away the barbarism of Louis XIV by citing the beauty of Versailles and its furniture. The same dual nature of Islam—the tension between compassion and tolerance on the one hand and exhortations to violent evangelism on the other—that had so compromised the achievements of the Arab empire still held sway under the Turks. The range of tortures, slow deaths, and persecutions devised by the new guardians of Islam for many unbelievers, as well as for Muslims of rival factions, became widespread and infamous enough to ensure that both the Ottoman and the Mughal empires would be forever plagued by fractiousness and, occasionally, outright rebellions. The greatness of their cultural achievements is indeed undeniable; but how much greater their achievements might have been had they been able to finally recognize the anachronistic nature of many of the Koran's most violent passages—and thereby tap the full constructive and creative potential of *all* their subjects—no one can say. Like Rome, the Ottoman and Mughal were empires that did not reach dizzying heights *because* of their brutality; they reached them *despite* it, and their eventual decay and collapse was hastened in no small measure because of their identification as ruthless, repressive regimes, and because of the vengeful willingness of many of their own citizens to participate in their toppling.

But indigenous, self-defeating brutality was not restricted to the great Christian and Muslim powers of the world, as European colonists had already discovered in the New World. Few events had demonstrated the ultimate costs of destructive war more than the Aztec collapse after the arrival of the Spanish in Mexico a century earlier. That noteworthy society had been done in as much by the defection of fellow Indian tribes that they had long brutalized as it had by Spanish firearms and European diseases. In the wake of the Spanish campaigns of annihilation in Central and South America, not only

Spanish but English and French colonists were to learn
that similarly hard rules of life obtained in North America.

Often romanticized as peaceful tribes who knew little
of systematic cruelty until the Europeans came, Indian
nations such as the Iroquois and tribes such as the Algon-
quin taught the European newcomers their own vicious
techniques of destructive war learned during generations
of conflict with one another. Certainly it is true that the
Europeans quickly enlisted these tribes to fight in their
own colonial conflicts, hoping to use their indigenous
tactics of terror to frighten opposing settlers off the continent. It is also true that during these encounters, the
Europeans shared their own time-honored methods of
ravaging civilian populations with the Indians. But as
should have been learned long ago in the Old World,
changing the particular method of destructive war did
nothing to alter its effect. More often than not, indiscriminate Indian violence against white settlers became a
spur to defiance, rather than a cause of withdrawal. And
once again, attempting to use the agents of such terrifying
depredations for one's own purposes led to those agents
being well-positioned to turn against their supposed masters and do immense damage, as British and French colonial
administrators learned during the two powers' periodic
wars against each other on the American frontier.

Thus by the close of the seventeenth century, destructive war and the tactics of terror had attained a truly

global scope, through a wide variety of agents: international affairs did not at all resemble the hopeful dreams of Grotius and the other jurists. But there was one philosopher active at the time who did seem to have his finger on the true and racing pulse of the world, though his analyses of the violence around him were so unblinking, even stark, that many philosophical scholars (who, like other cultural didacts, tend to find ways to overlook or rationalize brutality when it interferes with a more aesthetically oriented view of human history) have relegated him to the second tier of great thinkers. But since accurate dissection of one's times and surroundings, along with frank prescriptions for their ills, must be considered valid measures of true philosophical insight, Thomas Hobbes deserves to be given as much respect as any seventeenth-century thinker.

Writing in England during that nation's civil war, Hobbes had originally intended his work to be a defense of King Charles I's right to rule absolutely in order to maintain a regulated and peaceful society. But when Charles was revealed as unequal to this task, Hobbes generalized his statements to declare that *any* ruler or group of rulers could prove their legitimacy by effectively maintaining social cohesion and quelling disorder. Well versed in the emerging science of psychology, Hobbes did not accept the idea that man's actions are at bottom determined by his desire to avoid pain and experience pleasure;

man's first desire, he said, is security, and pleasure can be sacrificed, and pain endured, if such security is the reward. The most common identification of the path to security, of course—for the average person as well as for nations—is the aggregation of power, which Hobbes considered a pragmatic rather than a gratuitous drive.

"I put for a general inclination of mankind," he wrote in his masterwork, *Leviathan,* "a perpetual and restless desire of power after power, that ceaseth only in death. And the cause of this, is not always that a man hopes for more intensive delight than he has already attained to; or that he cannot be content with a more moderate power; but because he cannot assure the power and means to live well, which he hath present, without the acquisition of more." Power, and hence security, are thus ever receding goals; the pursuit of these unattainable objects drives men to such perpetual madness as was consuming the world in the seventeenth century. Therefore it was pointless to discuss notions concerning international legal organizations unless one first discussed what force was to support them—for that force would have to be more ruthless and powerful than that of any potential disrupters of international stability.

"Covenants, without the sword," Hobbes said, "are but words, and of no strength to secure a man at all. The bonds of words are too weak to bridle men's ambition, avarice, anger and other passions, without the fear of some coercive power." There was only one such power: the state, the overbearing but protective "leviathan," which must be viewed as a "Mortal God, to which we owe under the Immortal God, our peace and defence." (Among other things, Hobbes's theories endorsed the final subordination of church to state in England that had begun with Henry VIII and Elizabeth I.) Hobbes's central lesson was to prove an eternal one, and it bears enormous implications for the fight against terrorism today: in the same way that only the punishing power, the "sword," of the state can keep citizens from breaking their social "covenant" with one another, only nations that raise well-armed, progressively trained, and above all highly disciplined armies—and are prepared to use those armies to inflict what we would today call decisive (not merely massive) retaliation against disruptive countries—offer the practical hope of maintaining international order.

By analyzing politics, history, and military force through the lens of psychology, Hobbes established a perspective on human affairs that went largely unappreciated or misunderstood in his own day, and indeed has never received the universal appreciation it deserves. Much attention has instead been paid to some of his darker aphorisms, most notably his comment that the insecurities of mankind, and the competition for power that is produced by them, ensure that most people's lives are "solitary, poor, nasty, brutish, and short." But such statements are impossible to understand outside the context of the decades of destructive war through which Hobbes lived. And while many of Hobbes's more complex ideas were too radically advanced to be implemented by the usual stripe of viciously acquisitive seventeenth-century leader, they did find at least one exponent, although not the one Hobbes had originally envisioned: it was Oliver Cromwell and his New Model Army, not Charles I and his addled notions about divine monarchy, that bore out the Hobbesian theory that a ruler or faction could claim legitimacy only by demonstrating the ability to enforce the laws of the land and guarantee security to the people. But Cromwell's experience was never truly emulated outside England during Hobbes's lifetime (even by Cromwell himself). It was to take the dawn of a new era and the arrival of a new breed of rulers for such forceful yet effective methods of controlling destructive war to be implemented in Europe. And even after the practice of ensuring peace and the safety of ordinary citizens by establishing professional, politically disinterested, and highly disciplined armies became widespread on that continent, there was no certainty at all that it would prove effective against the generalized violence that was continuing to afflict much of the rest of the world.

CHAPTER FIVE

HONOR HAS NO EFFECT ON THEM

History offers few examples of political and philosophical leaders more inclined toward self-promotion, or more convinced of their own importance to posterity, than those of eighteenth-century Europe. The great minds of the Enlightenment believed that everything they thought about, wrote about, or had administration over was the better for their attention, and the conduct of war was no exception; indeed, in this area they did their work particularly well, for eighteenth-century Europe has retained a reputation as a place in which international conflict was governed by an extraordinarily civilized set of rules, a code that came to be known by the hopeful term "limited war." According to this doctrine, wars could only really "succeed" (in the sense of avoiding generalized, mutually devastating destruction) if they were fought not by entire tribes or nations in pursuit of the unconditional surren-

der and complete prostration of the enemy (as had been
the case since the days of the Romans) but rather by professional armies whose leaders were after specific and
limited political goals—principles first espoused by the
Italian *condottieri*. The rebirth and propagation of these
ideas did indeed drastically reduce the effects of warfare
on civilians between the eras of Louis XIV and Napoleon;
in fact (according to the *Oxford English Dictionary*), it
was in 1766 that the word *civilian* was first used to con-
note "noncombatant," a bit of information that no self-
respecting Enlightenment figure would have dismissed as
coincidence.

As with most things in Enlightenment Europe, this
passion for limited war proved as much a self-interested
fashion as a substantively altruistic philosophy. Unlike
most trends of the time, however, this one was at least set
by a figure whose achievements transcended mere words
(though he was a more-than-capable writer, as well). King
Frederick II of Prussia, whose ideas and exploits would
win for him the sobriquet *Great,* in 1740 took the throne
of a kingdom that just half a century earlier had been
forged out of various second-rate German states. Prussia
was still far from secure, being surrounded by hungry nations whose elaborate courtly rituals did little to hide
their lust for power and territory. But the contemplative
Frederick had inherited a strong, proficient army from his
father, a severe man and parent who would have been

more surprised than anyone had he known that with this instrument, his son would set the example and conduct the campaigns that would give real meaning to the concept of "limited war" in Europe.

It may be true that Frederick's image as a monarch who felt deep compassion for and identification with his subjects has been overstated; though more plainly dressed and plainly spoken than his royal counterparts in other countries, he did prize his friendship with such *philosophes* as Voltaire as much as any of them. Yet his statement that "Useful hardworking people should be guarded as the apple of one's eye, and in wartime recruits should be levied in one's own country only when the bittersweet necessity compels" has the distinct ring of earnestness. And, qualified as such concern for his subjects might have been, it nonetheless constituted a more progressive view than anything the world had seen in a ruler since Oliver Cromwell. By moving beyond the principles of both Cromwell and the *condottieri,* Frederick devised the most powerful statement and proof yet that wars were best fought for particular and realistic political goals by soldiers whose restrained behavior would limit the impact of conflict on civilians and thereby maintain or even win those citizens' loyalty. There were other military commanders of equal battlefield acumen during the eighteenth century, and a few of these even understood the need to avoid alienating civilians: Marshal Hermann (later Maurice) Saxe, the German mercenary who saved France during the 1740s, and General James Wolfe, the brilliant Englishman who gave his life destroying France's power in North America during the French and Indian War, stand out as particular examples. But neither of these men was in a position to establish the global precedent that Frederick the Great could and did. Thus it is to Frederick that most of the credit for reforming European war in the eighteenth century belongs.

It should be understood, however, that the Prussian king achieved this distinction by displaying as much contempt for his soldiers as he did compassion for his citizens. But then, the traditionally abysmal behavior of European fighting men scarcely permitted any other attitude for a commander interested in advancing the principles of progressive war. Immediately on taking his throne, Frederick demonstrated his ideas about conflict by seizing the province of Silesia from Austria in a campaign that was remarkably quick, confined, and respectful of civilian lives and property. Like Cromwell, Frederick depended on one policy above all to secure his military, and thereby his social, successes: discipline. His soldiers were, to begin with, forced to wear even more elaborate and distinguishable uniforms than Cromwell's had been, and they could be punished severely for removing them while on duty. Thus accoutred, they were watched by their superiors night and day, and under no circumstances were they allowed to "forage" (history's most common euphemism for plundering) on their own. Desertion became a dire offense, for Frederick knew that most soldiers did not desert because they were homesick but rather to gain a chance to use the weapons he'd given them to do a little "foraging" on their own. This rule eventually became so strict in Frederick's army that troops were often not allowed to bathe or even to go to the latrine unaccompanied. "The slightest loosening of discipline," the king declared, thinking of the excesses of a century earlier, "would lead to barbarization." Soldiers had not changed over time and likely never would: "Therefore (since honor has no effect on them) they must fear their officers more than any danger." Discipline even influenced tactics: soldiers went into action in tightly formed units, where they could be seen at all times, and the army rarely marched at night.

Frederick balanced these extreme views with progressive policies concerning pay, medical care, and quartering; but the quality that most ensured his men's loyalty, in spite of all the exacting discipline they had to endure, was his aversion to costly pitched battles. "It is to be remarked," Frederick explained, "that most generals in love with battle resort to this expedient for want of other resources." Given that Prussia was surrounded by larger, wealthier countries—any one of which, in the eighteenth-century diplomatic world of ever shifting alliances, could become an enemy at a moment's notice—avoiding large battles was not just a matter of personal inclination: it was also strategically and fiscally prudent. He therefore replaced the old martial virtue of trying to engage the enemy and utterly destroy him with an emphasis on position, on maneuvering an opponent into a hopeless situation without assaulting him, usually through carefully planned offensive marches that were preemptive in nature, and aimed at achieving shocking surprise.

As time went by, other European powers attempted to replicate Frederick's successes by employing professional armies that contained large contingents of mercenaries. Further following the Prussian example, these nations showed little inclination to squander such resources on doomed attempts to resist once they had been outthought. And so battles of annihilation became fewer and even more gratuitous. "I perceive that small states can maintain themselves against the greatest monarchies," Frederick said, echoing the *condottieri,* "when these states put industry and a great deal of order into their affairs. I find that the great empires are full of abuses and confusion; that they maintain themselves only by their vast resources and by the intrinsic force of their mass."

The tone of such comments seems to foreshadow the attitude in our own time of various terrorist groups (as well as the governments that sponsor them) toward the United States and other wealthy nations of the West.

Furthermore, Frederick the Great's version of limited war, like many terrorist actions today, was seen at the time by many military traditionalists as a corrupted form of fighting. For such reactionary critics, "fair" and "honorable" combat involved set battles that produced absolute victory. But this idea was increasingly archaic, as well as increasingly expensive and unpopular with the millions of peasants who provided the levies and the material support for European armies. Frederick's style of war, on the other hand, though used to pursue ends that most peasants either did not understand or cared little about, was nonetheless immensely popular because of its limited impact on society as a whole. In the same way, international terrorism derives much of its popularity in the countries from which it springs because it obviates the need for most of their citizens to actually participate in combat.

Are there, then, ways in which terrorism is actually a progressive form of warfare? Some analysts think so (or did, before the September 11 attacks). And indeed, it must be acknowledged that, while terrorists have a fatal misunderstanding of their victims' mentalities and reactions, they understand those of their supporters quite well and are able to exploit the natural desire of such citizens to avoid participation in generalized conflict. Ironically, however, this lone sense in which terrorism is limited actually encompasses a horrific betrayal of those same supporters, for it is generally on such easily targetable citizens, rather than on the carefully hidden terrorist groups, that retaliation is inflicted.

For the people of Prussia—whose king in no way resembled a terrorist, promulgating as he did a concept of limited war that was not similarly perverse—there was never any question of such reprisals: Frederick won nearly every battle and conflict he entered, and he relentlessly expanded the power and borders of his kingdom. By the time of his death in 1786, Prussia had become a principal player in the emerging "European balance of power," while other kingdoms unable or unwilling to effectively implement Frederick's concept of progressive war had seen their power decline, as in the case of Austria, or had been partitioned and disappeared entirely, as in the case of Poland. Here at last was an international demonstration of what Cromwell had proved within England: by refraining from destructive war a nation could advance its interests almost beyond imagining, whereas adherence to outdated tactics opened a path to national self-destruction.

Frederick's political goals—the strengthening and expansion of Prussia—were no more idealistic than those of any other European monarch. But his innovative policies *did* have a salutary effect on the collective health of the Continent by forcing other powers to intimidate him, if only as a method of checking his rise. Thus, the image of Prussia as a savage, warlike country—one propagated largely by nations such as France, which were ostensibly more refined but in fact far more destructive—was from the first unfair, to say nothing of inaccurate. For it was in Prussia that progressive war was, for all practical international purposes, truly born; and it is progressive war—limited, pegged to specific political goals, sparing of civilian life, and reliant on daring offensive action to resolve dangerous situations before they develop into overwhelmingly violent ones—that offers the best hope for prosecuting modern war, particularly the war against terrorism.

The effects of this new military and social thinking were by no means limited to the arena of global politics. Frederick's theories and actions had a deep impact on the ongoing effort of jurists to define new and better codes of conduct for international relations. Indeed, it is difficult not to detect traces of the Prussian king's philosophy in the work of the greatest jurist of the eighteenth (and perhaps of any other) century, Emmerich de Vattel, who in 1758 published his enormously influential study, *The Law of Nations.*

The son of a Swiss pastor, Vattel was, like Frederick, realistic in a way that held out the promise of more tangible good than all the idealism of his more high-minded contemporaries. Breaking ranks not only with influential Enlightenment philosophers of war and peace, such as

John Locke, but also with scholars of the early and late
Middle Ages, such as St. Augustine and Thomas Aquinas,
Vattel advanced the shocking idea that it is pointless to
talk about which cause in a given war is just; every party
believes its own to be and can almost never be shaken
from that conviction. The true indicator of which side
carries the right, Vattel continued, is not the relative
merit of antebellum claims but something much easier to
assess and judge: the behavior of belligerents *during* actual hostilities. "Thus," he declared, "the rights founded
on the state of war, the lawfulness of its effects, the validity of acquisition made by arms, do not, externally and
between mankind, depend on the justice of the cause, but
on the legality of the means in themselves."

There remained, of course, the problem of defining a
"legal means" of making war; and yet there already existed
a consensus on the subject among the citizens of Europe,
as well as, increasingly, among many of their leaders. "All
damage done to the enemy unnecessarily," Vattel said,
"[and] every act of hostility which does not tend to procure victory and bring the war to a conclusion, is a licen-
tiousness condemned by the law of nature." But what
about those proponents of destructive war who believed
that their depredations against civilians, their tactics of
terror, did indeed "tend to procure victory"? Vattel acknowledged the difficulty of this point, asking, "How

then shall we, in particular cases, determine with precision, to what lengths it was necessary to carry hostilities in order to bring the war to a happy conclusion? And even if the point could be ascertained," he went on, pinpointing the eternal dilemma of international jurists, "nations acknowledge no common judge: each forms her own judgment of the conduct she is pursuing to fulfill her duties. If you once open a door for continual accusation of outrageous excess in hostilities, you will only augment the number of complaints, and influence the minds of the contending parties with increasing animosity: fresh injuries will be perpetually springing up; and the sword will never be sheathed till one of the parties be utterly destroyed."

Without knowing it, this relatively obscure jurist from a pleasant Swiss town was predicting the course that war—and its legal ramifications—would take over the next 250 years. But did he have an answer to the dilemma he had described? He did—though it would never be vigorously applied. Vattel's proposal for judging what constituted injustice during wartime was to disallow any contextual rationalizations and deviations: there could be no extenuating circumstances when it came to the violation of international rules of bellicose conduct arrived at by a consensus of nations. These rules should therefore be carefully formulated, so that they would be "sure and easy in the application." Echoing Grotius, Vattel declared that these rules must apply to both aggressor and aggrieved, since, again, discussions of whose cause was just were irrelevant. Such uniform application of a set of mutually agreed upon rules would, of course, lead to most wars being ended by compromise, and Vattel applauded this, asserting, "A treaty of peace can be no more than a compromise."

Vattel's suggestions were not airtight—there was still ample room for abuse if the nations charged with righting mutually determined wrongs did not act in a unified, forceful manner to punish the violators. But the idea that injustice in war was to be determined by behavior rather than by relative merits was deeply important, and holds enormous resonance for our current struggle against terrorism. As stated earlier, the quest to counter terrorism, both diplomatically and militarily, has sparked the creation of rafts of documents and hours of programming devoted to weighing the relative justness or unjustness of the causes for which the nations and peoples from which terrorists spring are struggling. Yet if terrorism is to be eradicated, "Vattel's law"—that certain belligerent behaviors are beyond questions of justness and even rob just causes of their rectitude—must be applied. And when it is, we can see that we will in fact never eliminate terrorism if we try to determine our response to it by weighing the merits of various specific terrorist causes. *All* terrorists

and terrorist sponsors must be treated, uniformly and severely, as factions and nations whose behavior has nulli-
fied any justness that they might have otherwise claimed
for their cause—as people and nations, in short, who
have declared themselves to be at war not with any particular country or coalition but with civilization itself.
(Thus, Osama bin Laden's assertion that, say, American
bases should be removed from Muslim holy ground may
be just; but bin Laden's *methods* are only undermining
that justness.)

It was Vattel who most effectively illuminated this
critical lesson of a uniform, forceful response to any and
all unacceptable belligerent behavior during wartime, just
as it was Frederick the Great who most effectively demonstrated why such a forceful response must always be
progressive—that is, perpetually on the offensive, using
surprise to achieve success, and above all breaking with
the vengeful, indiscriminately violent traditions of destructive war. That both of these lessons are two and a half
centuries old should not deter us from allowing our behavior to be informed by them, for the intervening generations have only demonstrated their merit. If we find,
however, that much of the world is unwilling to follow
such venerable advice, we should not be greatly surprised,
for the ideas of Frederick the Great and Vattel were controversial even in their own day. True, several of them had
an effect, for a time, in Europe, but Europe is not the

world, and as increasing numbers of its citizens chose to explore, trade with, and emigrate to other parts of the globe, they found themselves coming into routine contact with peoples, cultures, and situations that tested what strength they had to adhere to the progressive principles of Vattel and Frederick the Great—tested it, indeed, past the breaking point.

CHAPTER SIX

TO PREACH HATRED

During the eighteenth century, the first encounter with unlimited warfare that Europeans departing their homelands faced often took place on the sea itself. Piracy had, of course, been a constant characteristic of warfare since seaworthy ships had first been devised, but it was the rise of sixteenth-century privateers such as Drake—and the success of their raids aimed at the treasure ships and ports of the Spanish empire—that gave birth to the "golden age of piracy" in the seventeenth century. The label is undeniably misleading, for there was little about piracy that could accurately be called "golden" save the booty such very dubious characters coveted. Certainly, some pirates had enough character and charisma to inspire romantic legends, but these stories hold up roughly as well when matched against the historical record as do the *chansons de geste* of the Middle Ages. Even such appealing buccaneer leaders as Sir Henry Morgan, who built up a princely estate in Jamaica by repeatedly raiding important Spanish treasure ports, did not hesitate to allow their men to torture citizens en masse, kill and rape at will, and destroy property and crops whenever they saw fit.

Indeed, the piracy of the "golden age" bears at least a superficial resemblance to modern-day terrorism, particularly in the number of its variations: ships attacking ships, making commerce and travel a high-risk undertaking; official naval vessels impressing the sailors of neutral ships into service; and coastal raiding, which could result—as in the case of the city of Panama at Morgan's hands in 1671—in the fearsome eradication of entire civilian communities. Nor was such activity confined to the Spanish Main or, for that matter, to men: piracy infected every ocean and sea on the globe, and women occasionally appeared as featured players. The greatest of the latter was the remarkable Mrs. Cheng, who operated during the opening years of the nineteenth century in the South China Sea and eventually commanded thousands of pirates on board hundreds of vessels: more naval force than most countries could muster and one of the greatest piratical empires ever known.

Piracy, like so many forms of avaricious and occasionally pathological bloodlust, has been a source of endless fascination and romanticization in Western society, conjuring images of rogue ships crewed by drunken raiders preying on fat commercial vessels. But in truth piracy had evolved by the late seventeenth century into an organized and powerful form of random violence and theft that threatened one of the few established pillars of international law: freedom of the seas. The Barbary states of North Africa, for example—Muslim principalities that were loosely federated with the Ottoman empire—were whole nations built effectively on piracy, and by the late eighteenth century their activities could sometimes bring Mediterranean commerce to a virtual standstill. Such state-sponsored commerical enterprises were neither a romantic nor an amusing matter for the average traveler or merchant of the time.

Thus piracy does indeed bear many of the destructive hallmarks of modern terrorism and is, when recognized as an international organized threat, of some use in shedding light on our current situation. Of course, by the eighteenth century one key element of terrorism— indeed, *the* key element—had disappeared among pirates: the political objective. Piracy was no longer aimed at changing the political behavior of nations by attacking their commercial agents and their trade; its overall goal was simple theft, a goal achieved increasingly through kidnapping and the extortion of protection money as much as through armed robbery. Yet piracy's similarity to terrorism in method and effect was nonetheless so strong that at least one group of national leaders—those in the

United States during the first decades of the republic's existence—was eventually driven to the same conclusion that American leaders have apparently reached with regard to terrorism today: that such behavior could not (as it cannot now) be stopped by pursuing and arresting individual offenders and then trying them as criminals. Particularly in the case of the Barbary pirates, who not only had state sponsors but often amounted to the armed forces of those states, something much more was needed. Even so personally pacifist a president as Thomas Jefferson could see that a decisive offensive response by conventional military forces was required. Jefferson's dispatch in 1803 of a single warship to take care of the problem proved woefully inadequate (the vessel ran aground and its crew was taken hostage), but in 1815 a full naval squadron under Commodore Stephen Decatur sailed into the Mediterranean Sea, sinking Barbary ships, killing high Barbary officers and officials, and generally convincing the pirate states that the United States was better left alone.

If they *were* able to make it safely across the sea, whether to Asia, Africa, or the Americas, eighteenth-century Europeans were confronted with a fantastic array of societies and cultures, about all of which they could be reasonably sure of one thing: none of them were either acquainted with or had any use for the notion of limited war that was taking hold in Europe. For the eighteenth century was a time of enormous upheaval in almost every corner of the globe. Much of this turmoil was, without question, the result of European colonial and economic meddling, but an even greater portion was caused by long-standing ethnic and tribal rivalries, antagonisms so potent that many of them have survived into our own era.

In India, for example, it was certainly true that the various European commercial companies trading with the indigenous states regularly engaged in destabilizing economic exploitation under the protection of mercenary military forces (what were known as "merchant soldiers"). This problem was only aggravated when those companies were nationalized and backed by the power of European armies, as seen most notably in the case of the British East India Company. But it is also true that, had the main Indian states been able to put aside their internal feuding and rivalries long enough to mount a concerted effort to repel the Europeans, they would have had enough combined military might and skill to accomplish the task. Indeed, the ability of the British to exploit this divisiveness and buy the services of certain native leaders was a crucial component of their power to defeat others. Enlisting the aid of such supposed native allies, however, would eventually present them with the same problem that Roman and Muslim leaders had faced when they allowed barbarian and mercenary tribesmen into their legions.

Nor was the plight of such Indian states as Mysore,

the Maratha confederacy, and the declining Mughal empire made any easier by encroachment from the west by other non-Western powers. Persistent attempts by various Muslim potentates to invade India by way of Afghanistan plagued the principalities of the subcontinent during the eighteenth century. The greatest of these campaigns was launched by the dynamic and aggressive Nadir Shah, a Turcoman tribesman who had risen to assume power over the Safavid empire in Persia. Nadir penetrated the Mughal domain as far as Delhi, which he sacked, and he might have gone farther. Fortunately for the Indians, Nadir believed that it was his destiny to resolve the schism between Sunn'ism and Shi'ism that had long divided Islam, and in 1747 he was, like so many Muslims who had attempted to resolve the faith's deep internecine conflicts, assassinated. But the man who inherited the eastern portion of Nadir's kingdom, Ahmad Khan, kept up the southeastward pressure from Afghanistan, eventually annexing several Indian provinces and defeating the Maratha confederacy of Hindu tribes at the Battle of Panipat in 1761, one of the largest land engagements the world had ever known.

During all these campaigns, such rules as characterized European limited war were unknown—for, again, these were clashes of peoples, of tribes, and of religions, conflicts in which not only the enemy army but the entire opposing population was viewed as a legitimate target of military violence. In such conflicts, "conquest" nearly always meant massacre, torment, and destruction that was universal in scope and unrestrained in severity—an ominous precedent for the belligerent attitudes we hear expressed from the same region today.

European traders and missionaries bound for China, on the other hand, discovered a land where the weapons and troops were as yet equal to the tasks of securing and expanding the empire's borders and limiting foreign encroachment. But the Ch'ing, or Manchu, dynasty was no more interested in mitigating the effects of warfare on civilians than was any other Asian power of the time— indeed, the Manchus identified brutality with control, and they pursued their military campaigns with a harshness to equal any of their neighbors to the west. Ignoring, as every other imperial dynasty before them had, the admonishments of China's ancient sage of limited war, Sun-tzu—who advised that "the expert in using the military subdues the enemy's forces without going into battle, takes the enemy's walled cities without launching an attack, and crushes the enemy's state without a protracted war"—the Manchus and their military commanders consistently relied on the principle that terrorizing their subjects would make them obedient and docile.

By the early eighteenth century, the Manchus had established an extensive network of roads and communications to facilitate the task of subjugating Tibet, along with the last Mongol strongholds in the northwestern provinces of the empire and a range of other tribal enemies along various borders. These campaigns took the better part of the century; having completed them—as well as having already solved the ever vexing problem of Taiwan by conquering it in 1683—the Manchus could see no reason to be impressed by either Western military methods or Western ideas about how wars should be fought. True, their style of conquest meant that their new subjects periodically rose up in rebellion and that the heavily Muslim western provinces of the empire would never be entirely pacified (as indeed they are not today, explaining why China is so anxious to join the global coalition against Islamic fundamentalist terrorism), but such troublesome facts were not viewed by those who occupied and served the Dragon Throne in Beijing as cause for anything but tighter social control and more repressive military measures.

The Ottoman empire, meanwhile, was attempting a similarly repressive reaction to the increasing number of rebellious subjects within its borders, though there was a much greater sense of urgency about this work. Beset not only by internal malcontents but by enemy states on all sides who were anxious to dismember it, the empire was being swept into the general downward spiral that would lead to its being labeled "the sick man of Europe" in the next century. To the east, the Ottomans faced the forces of Nadir Shah and his heirs; in the south, there were repeated uprisings in Egypt and among the tribes of Arabia, rebellions that the Ottomans' harsh countermeasures only further inflamed. (In the wake of this repression by the Ottomans—who were perceived by many Arab Muslims as decadent, lax followers of Islam—religious fundamentalism began to gain many adherents among the Arabian tribes. It was at this time that the Wahhabi sect, spiritual forefathers of Osama bin Laden and his followers, took shape.) But the principal challenge facing Ottoman rulers was the ongoing effort of such varied European powers as Austria, Russia, and even the city-state of Venice to liberate Christian Europe from the "Turks" (as they were increasingly known, since their fellow Muslims had little desire to be associated with them). The most vicious parts of this struggle took place, predictably, in the Balkans; and it was not always the Turks who displayed the greatest barbarity.

In 1716, an Austrian army, having defeated a large Turkish force in a battle that heralded Austria's conquest of Hungary, slaughtered some thirty thousand Turkish troops: the strictures of limited war had not yet taken hold in what had always been, and would remain, one of the most brutal states in Europe. Russia, in the meantime, first conquered the khanate of the Crimea, then later marched on Bucharest, further diminishing Ottoman holdings in Europe. The greatest of these Russian victories were won by Count Peter Rumyantsev, a soldier whose ability to both effect surprise through innovative tactics and defeat drastically superior numbers of Turkish forces rivaled much of what Frederick the Great had achieved farther north. But warfare in the Balkans was even then a bitter business. Despite the obvious advantages of incorporating the progressive lessons being applied by Rumyantsev and others, the Turks instead relied ever more heavily on terrorizing the inhabitants of their remaining European provinces, committing horrific atrocities and massacres. Eventually these would be answered in kind, perpetuating the cycle of mass murder and reprisal that marks the behavior of Christians and Muslims in the region to this day.

As for Africa, the dominant aspect of eighteenth-century European interaction with that continent was, of course, the rabidly active slave trade. Historians have tended to depict this practice as simply brutal economic exploitation of one race by another; they overlook, perhaps for reasons of political correctness, the fact that had intertribal warfare on the African continent not been so common, and had the capture and sale of defeated warriors and civilians not been a standard element of that warfare, the region would have held comparatively few possibilities for Western slavers. Once again, indigenous varieties of destructive war opened the way for European manipulation and abuse. To portray the situation as one in which Africans had no responsibility fails to help us understand not only political and military realities in Africa today but also the hidden yet crucial effect that engaging in such activities was having on Europeans, especially European soldiers.

For what the Westerners initially failed, for the most part, to comprehend was that in order to first exploit and then master the violent situations in which they found themselves abroad, they had to understand the tactics of both their enemies and the native allies with whom they consorted. But as they reached this terrible understanding, the European soldiers and settlers also began to practice those same tactics, rationalizing their behavior with the infamous logic that "to defeat a savage one must become a savage." It is an argument, as already noted, that is often invoked today in the context of our war against terrorism; and it is just as self-serving and hollow now as it was 250 years ago. The idea that one cannot defeat those who practice the tactics of terror without practicing such tactics oneself has never been more than a fig leaf behind which naturally malicious, vengeful, and bloodthirsty characters attempt to hide their own barbarity. And the consequences of such shameful rationalizations are always disastrous: in the case of eighteenth-century Europeans, many of the progressive principles and techniques concerning the conduct of war that had been hammered out during long centuries of destructive war

began to fall away. Fighting beside and against native soldiers who knew nothing of such systematic ideas, Europeans more often than not reverted to behaviors that
still lay just beneath the civilized veneer of enlightened
eighteenth-century conduct. This reversion was seldom
openly acknowledged in the drawing rooms of the capi-
tals of Europe, but it was a corrosive agent that, once introduced, inexorably did its work, helping to prepare the
way for a collapse of the advances that had been so hard
won.

Nowhere was this process demonstrated more clearly
than in North America. Terror had always held a valued
position in the military tactics of most North American
Indian tribes, and the practice was not always gratuitous:
nomadic tribes are never so populous as settled agrarian
peoples, and by achieving their political goals through
terrorizing rather than engaging their enemies, such
tribes lost far fewer warriors. Ritualized violence was,
simply put, a way to achieve the maximum psychological
effect (for the violent depredations committed by Indian
tribes against one another were indeed horrifying) with
the minimum number of cataclysmic battles. Such ex-
planations were lost, however, on most European newcomers, who knew only that they had never personally
witnessed such depths of bloody indulgence among their
own people. In effect, when it came to white settlers and
traders, Indian tactics of terror did their job too well.

Deeply traumatized by what they saw and experienced, whites learned quickly to match or exceed Indian outrages, and not just for psychological or exemplary purposes—anti-Indian European terror in America was aimed first at removal and later at extermination.

Thus the tactics of terror played, from the beginning, a sinister role in the development of white civilization in the New World, giving birth to an unacknowledged moral and psychological duality that was only to grow over time. Among themselves, Westerners were capable of formulating and expressing tremendously admirable principles concerning individualism, liberty, and participatory government; but when it came to the treatment of Indian tribes and other dangerous elements, internal and external, these principles were considered void and non-binding. In place of Vattel's progressive thoughts on compromise with opponents came far more regressive ideas about the absolute defeat and eradication of enemies.

The corrupting influence of this duality was only aggravated by the fact that from time to time both white settlers and white soldiers in America found it necessary to ally themselves with various Indian tribes in order to combat their own Western imperial rivals. This condition reached its high point during the French and Indian War, which broke out in 1754 and saw Britain and its Indian allies pitted against France and her more numerous native cohorts. From the beginning, the French—who had fewer settlements in America and thus less ability to sustain large numbers of regular troops—relied more heavily on the Indian tribes. For several reasons, this reliance played a significant part in their defeat and subsequent elimination as an effective power on the continent. First and most evident, the vicious raids that the French-backed Indians felt emboldened (and were encouraged by their allies) to launch against settlers in British colonies had the usual effect not of breaking the settlers' spirits but of stiffening their resolve. Then, too, the Indians tended to be very capricious allies, ready to desert at the smallest slight or perceived insult—a fact that, in conjunction with their taste for slaughtering civilians, led such exceptionally talented and unusually ethical British leaders in America as General James Wolfe to regard them with the gravest suspicion and distaste and to limit their deployment.

The French, however, could not afford the luxury of such scruples: their cause depended on the participation of their allies, and so even French commanders who knew, or should have known, better—most notably Wolfe's famous counterpart in Canada, the Marquis de Montcalm—were forced to countenance the Indians' counterproductive looting and murder raids. Ultimately, France's North American fate bore out the principle that those who rely most heavily on the tactics of terror will see their interests suffer the more: following Wolfe's stunning defeat of Montcalm at Quebec in 1759, the French never again asserted themselves seriously in America (although they did not depart altogether until the sale of their remaining possessions to the United States in 1803).

But it should not be thought that the British forces had not also been deeply changed by their years of campaigning on the forbidding American frontier. Even James Wolfe, whose general orders to his troops for the Quebec expedition exhibited both a remarkable understanding of the principles of progressive war and a sensitivity to the plight of noncombatants, was not completely unaffected by the tactics to which his time in America had exposed him: though he emphasized discipline above all things, forbidding his men to burn churches or houses wantonly and declaring that "if any violence is offer'd to a woman, the offender shall be punish'd with death," Wolfe permitted the practice of scalping "when the enemy are Indians, or Canad[ian]s dressed like Indians."

It should have come as no surprise, then, that when the American Revolution broke out more than a decade after the conclusion of the French and Indian War, there were signs that the North American breed of destructive war was to play a strong part in the conflict. True, George Washington—who, like so many revolutionary officers, had served with the British army during the French and

Indian War—tried hard to instill tough discipline in his troops. Indeed, so concerned was he to avoid the excesses that he had witnessed while fighting the French on the frontier that he eventually imported mercenaries—most famously Baron Friedrich von Steuben, a German who had served in Frederick the Great's army—to assist in the task of drilling his men. Von Steuben's efforts met with creditable success among Washington's regulars, but it had already become plain that the characteristic colonial duality between lofty spoken principles and a willingness to employ harsh and even vicious methods against enemy soldiers and civilians (to say nothing of the freed slaves and Indians who fought with the British) had only intensified in the years since the defeat of the French.

Both rebels and loyalists were afflicted by this phenomenon. Especially in New York State and, later and even more intensely, during the southern campaigns that eventually culminated in the Battle of Yorktown, attacks on civilians who held opposing views were conducted not only by regular troops but by bands of irregular fighters who roamed the countryside, often using the war as a mere excuse for plunder, rape, and murder. As Nathanael Greene, one of the rebel commanders who worked hardest to limit such behavior, wrote to Alexander Hamilton from South Carolina in 1781, "Nothing has been more destructive to the true interest of this Country, than the mode adopted for its defence." Greene elaborated this thought in a letter written to his wife at the same time: "The sufferings and distress of the Inhabitants beggars all description, and requires the liveliest imagination to conceive the cruelties and devastations which prevail."

This is not a side of the American Revolution that has ever received a great deal of attention, for obvious reasons; yet it is the side that, for the purpose of understanding the roots not only of modern international terrorism but also of the American response to it, is the most important. For while soldiers of both the Continental and British armies had been accustomed to sustaining and committing breaches of eighteenth-century rules of limited war during their struggle with Indian tribes and the French (who could never quite be trusted to observe such rules, even in Europe), to be faced with such behavior on the part of former comrades and, until recently, fellow nationals was shocking. But no sense of moral indignation stopped either side from answering such tactics in kind: once again, outrage led only to imitative reprisals. These tales of atrocity were invariably exaggerated by both sides, but the fact that such acts were committed at all bore terrible witness to the fact that, in the realm of armed conflict, the continent of North America had imprinted the European settlers and soldiers far more than they had imprinted it. One of the clearest indications of this was the repeated (and ultimate) American call for unconditional surrender by the British—an idea that not only flew in the face of any notions of international law as promulgated by Grotius and Vattel but pointed ahead to an American tradition of similarly uncompromising, and therefore unusually brutal and desperate, conflicts.

The same duality bred in the American character by the perceived need to fight savages with savage methods, having already tainted the prosecution of a war against former fellow colonists and once friendly troops, next infected the formation of a new government. Indeed, there could have been no better expression of that duality than the Declaration of Independence itself, which promised all the liberating fruits of the Enlightenment to colonial white men but silently assented to continued bondage for blacks, destructive war against Indians, and few if any rights for women. All of this was rationalized by the need to do what was necessary and practical to get the new government established and to vanquish its various foes; from the beginning, the United States was prepared to compromise its internal principles in the pursuit of unconditional triumph over its external enemies. Yet as we have seen, this was not simply a consequence of the revolution itself: the two-tracked morality that permeated American affairs predated that conflict by many generations and was to outlast it by many more.

Back in Europe, meanwhile, the relative improvement

in the health of the Continent brought about by the ideas behind limited, progressive war was threatened by the success of the American cause. The French and Indian War had, of course, been but one part of a global conflict between France and England at the time—what was called in Europe the Seven Years War—and the regressive behavior of European soldiers that occurred in North America was echoed in many other theaters of that war's operations. France's final defeat had bred a popular desire for revenge against England that played a strong part in the French decision to aid the American rebels, an alliance that ultimately made American victory possible. French soldiers and sailors fought alongside the Continental army and navy in many engagements, and although it is impossible to determine how much this exposure to American radicals and their ideas exacerbated the French flirtation with notions of liberty and governmental reform (if not yet revolution), that the experience had *some* effect is undeniable. Perhaps by coincidence (though it would be an extraordinary one), when revolution finally did come to France, it also took the form of an unconditional affair—indeed, it proved even more uncompromising than the American war for independence had been. In the European future shaped by the French Revolution lay conflicts and terrors beyond the scope of anything seen on that continent in generations, not sim-

ply because of their utterly unlimited violence but because of their careful formulation. For the first time, an
educated set of European combatants—the leaders of
revolutionary France—sat down and codified the tactics
of terror, rather than merely unleashing them.

One of the earliest, and in many ways the clearest,
embodiments of this development was the infamous Article 1 of the mass conscription order passed by the
French National Convention in August 1793 in response
to proroyalist military intervention by outside powers:
"All Frenchmen," the document declared, "are perma-
nently requisitioned for service in the armies.

> The young men shall fight; the married men shall
> forge weapons and transport supplies; the women
> will make tents and clothes and will serve in the
> hospitals; the children will make up old linen into
> lint; the old men will have themselves carried into
> the public squares to rouse the courage of the fight-
> ing men, to preach the unity of the Republic and
> hatred against Kings.
>
> The public buildings shall be turned into bar-
> racks, the public squares into munition factories,
> the earthen floors of cellars shall be treated with lye
> to extract saltpetre.
>
> All firearms of suitable calibre shall be turned

over to the troops: the interior [of the country] shall be policed with shotguns and with cold steel.

All saddle horses shall be seized for the cavalry; all draft horses not employed in cultivation will draw the artillery and supply wagons.

Every element of society, then, was expected to specifically and explicitly turn its energies toward the prosecution of a national military effort. In so doing, all elements would, whether they realized it or not, make themselves potential targets for enemy retaliation. As the British historian and military theorist J.F.C. Fuller later observed, "Such was the birth-cry of total war."

Total war: to our ears the words sound unremarkable, for humanity has lived with the concept for two hundred years. And yet total war was not, at the time of its supposed inception, a step into the future; rather, it was a return to the unlimited wars of medieval and early modern Europe, a return even to the warfare of barbarian tribes. It was conflict without strictures or bounds, conflict in which the progressive ideas hammered out by soldiers and jurists over the centuries were among the first casualties. All too soon, Europe was once again a place in which no person was beyond the reach of attack in time of war. But why? What could possibly induce such learned, sophisticated human beings as those who formulated the principles of the French Revolution to throw away the precious few advances in belligerent conduct that had been achieved?

It was all done, in 1793 as it would be for generations to come, not in the name of a king, nor of a religion, nor even, truly, of a country. It was done in the name of an idea. The idea of the moment was liberty: in one of history's most terrible ironies, the cry for freedom that had been sparked by righteous, justified rage over the excesses of France's ruling elite unleashed a form of war that was to become the most destructive ever known. In return for the liberties promised by the revolution, every French citizen was expected to either kill or facilitate the killing of the enemies of the revolution and of the revolutionary state. Neither the English nor the American rebellions against monarchical authority had played with such fierce popular fire—and wisely so. For partisan passions in France would quickly make short work of the very ideals that had inspired the revolution, along with almost all other progressive or even coherent thought.

The resulting conflict—both within France and throughout Europe—assumed a life of its own, eventually becoming so consuming, so uncompromising, indeed so *total*, that mere ideas would no longer have the power to control it. Ultimately, it would take the firm hand of dictatorship—empty of any thought or philosophy more sophisticated than the cult of personal power—

to even begin to control the tumultuous violence. Yet even so strong a hand as Napoleon Bonaparte's would likely have been unable to completely tame such a juggernaut, assuming he had been able to put his own ego aside long enough to attempt it. Rather, he rechanneled the force of the mayhem into his own service, thereby extending the term of its terrible dominance. Only the utter prostration of the French nation itself finally wrote an end to more than twenty years of war in which assaults on populations were once again viewed as one of the most effective ways to affect the policies of princes and of legislatures.

Total war, then, was simply the successor to destructive war—nothing more or less than the new name for the tactics of terror. Making war on civilians for political purposes had entered the modern age, but its most basic lesson, demonstrated with rare fury on the French people, remained the same: the nation or group that first unleashed such tactics was destined to suffer their cruelties to a greater extent than anyone else.

CHAPTER SEVEN

VIOLENCE TO
ITS UTMOST BOUNDS

Before Napoleon's vain, almost apocalyptic plans for continental domination brought the wrath of most of Europe down on the French people, the Corsican cannoneer-turned-emperor had demonstrated to the world the extent to which the energies released by the French Revolution had made a new style of war possible. Yet it was not only the willingness of France's citizens to fight for an ideal (albeit an ever shifting one) that brought success to their nation's campaigns between 1792 and 1815. A second factor that set the French army apart was Napoleon's ability to harness its fervent emotion, to subject his "popular" army to the kind of martial discipline that had worked so well for Cromwell and Frederick the Great, and the reciprocal willingness of the French to submit themselves to such intense rigors. This discipline produced a national army of enormous proportions and intensity of feeling that could execute complex orders of battle—all in all, an unprecedented and fearsome machine.

But off the drilling ground and the battlefield, Napoleon proved less interested in disciplining his men: his army relied on foraging to achieve independence of movement during its campaigns, and the emperor was, as always, oblivious to the suffering that the average European noncombatant might experience as a result of any of his policies. The rest of the Continent's hatred of Napoleon is often explained by his apologists and devotees as arising from the reactionary European ancien régimes' fear of his dynamic new principles of war and government. But hatred of Napoleon was hardly confined to aristocrats, for his subordination of all other human activities to the needs of his army had an effect equal to any deliberate targeting of civilians. Many were the Prussian, Austrian, Italian, Spanish, and Russian soldiers and citizens who had bitter personal reasons for wanting to invade France and exact vengeance from the nation that had released so monstrously destructive an ego on the world.

Some peoples subjugated by Napoleon proved unable to wait, however, for that invasion to begin before striking back. In Calabria, the Tyrol, and especially Portugal and Spain, significant native resistance movements sprang up, striking for the most part from the shadows against

French officers and troops of occupation. These movements were acting less in support of any indigenous
regime or cause than out of a resentment of the French
presence, but they fought with real determination. Indeed, so intense did the combat become in these smaller-
scale encounters that in Spain they were dubbed
guerrillas—"small wars." The rebels who conducted such
campaigns eventually took the name for themselves, and
a new form of warfare, one that would have enormous
implications for civilians, was thus institutionalized.

Many analysts have likened guerrillas to modern-
day terrorists, with some reason. Guerrillas have always
tended to hide among civilian populations and to
draw support from them, as do terrorists. Also, reprisals from the conventional troops that guerrillas attack
have been inflicted on those civilians as much as or more
than on the guerrillas themselves. But it is precisely this
difference—of intended targets—that has usually sepa-
rated guerrillas from terrorists. The greatest masters and
theorists of guerrilla war have understood the need to
maintain the loyalty of the civilian population (a need
eventually codified by Mao Zedong in his famous "three
rules and eight remarks") and therefore have advised trying to limit casualties among noncombatants. It is an
overall strategy that has garnered almost as much success
as terrorism has failure: not only do civilians appreciate

the unusual consideration offered by capable guerrilla leaders, but they often admire the daring it takes for un- conventional units to attack regular troops. For terrorists, on the other hand, civilians *are* the target: terrorism's goal is to create fear among the enemy population, and its agents display remarkably little concern about the possi- bility of retaliation against the populations from which they themselves spring, cynically calculating that such re- taliation will breed a desire for revenge that will gain them increased public support.

Therefore, the similarities between guerrilla war and terrorist campaigns cannot ultimately be considered as important as their differences. Far more significant is the similarity of reaction that both groups inspire in their op- ponents. We have seen that the tactics of terror often bring about retaliatory strikes that themselves amount to terrorist acts, often targeting civilian communities. In at- tempting to respond to guerrilla activity, those same armed forces often commit precisely the same sort of acts: the usual strategy for countering guerrilla groups is to try to root them out from under the cover afforded by their presumed civilian sponsors through the use of indiscrim- inate brutality. From the French during the Napoleonic Wars through the responses of various governments to guerrilla movements in our own time, the torturing and killing of noncombatants suspected of harboring guerrillas has proved the usual but nevertheless the most ineffective way to curb their activities. Indeed, more often than not it only encourages popular support for such unconventional forces.

This pattern of misguided violence can all too often become cyclical: guerrilla forces that have sustained losses and setbacks, fired by the desire for revenge, periodically switch tactics and launch campaigns against civilians in desperate attempts to forcefully guarantee loyalty and control. At such times they see their efficacy erode precipitously; they also move, effectively, from the category of guerrillas to that of terrorists, subsequently reaping the meager rewards and the plentiful punishments that the tactics of terror have always offered. We have seen many examples of this transformation throughout history (the degeneration of the tactics of the Irish Republican Army during the early twentieth century is perhaps the most tragic and devastating case), and we continue to witness many more today. The shifts in activities and choices of victims by the various guerrilla and narco-guerrilla organizations in South America; the increasingly terrorist activities of Chechen partisans; and above all the change in the tactics on the part of those Palestinians participating in the *intifada* movement, away from attacking Israeli soldiers to blowing up Israeli civilians—all of these cases and others bear out the assertion that the easiest way for guerrillas to lose support both at home and internationally is to make the seemingly convenient but ultimately self-defeating decision to cross the slender, troublesome line that separates guerrilla war from terrorist campaign.

The guerrilla resistance to Napoleon in Spain and Portugal played an important supporting role in the victory of the conventional forces under the command of Britain's Duke of Wellington on the Iberian peninsula, a campaign that was vital to the overall defeat of Bonapartist France. This result was far more meaningful than anything ever achieved by deliberate warfare against civilians, and in itself illustrates the differences in methods and potential rewards between guerrilla and terrorist tactics. Napoleon's ultimate defeat at Waterloo in 1815 and his subsequent exile was not sufficient, however, to discourage the growth of a troubling cult of personality that was focused on the deposed emperor. Certain members of that cult came not from France but from countries formerly hostile to the French; indeed, some even came, after 1815, from enemy armies. More than a few soldiers retained a powerful fascination with the man they saw as the most accomplished member of their profession since Julius Caesar. But unlike Caesar, Napoleon had not been a noted chronicler or interpreter of his own exploits and ideas. That function was to be served by an intensely Romantic young officer of moderate notoriety but great literary interests and talent—a man who had served most of his career, ironically, in the Prussian army.

Karl von Clausewitz was far more than just another acolyte of Napoleon: he took Napoleon's ideas about total war and spun his own escalating variation on them, promulgating a set of principles that he generalized under the heading "absolute war." Having fought the French first as a Prussian staff officer and then, after Prussia was defeated, as a volunteer seconded to the Russian tsar's forces, Clausewitz was deeply committed not only to defeating the French but to making sure that his own country learned to fight with methods that were even more Napoleonic than Napoleon's own had been. Essentially an intellectual, Clausewitz determined that the best way for him to achieve this result was to write down his thoughts about the French emperor's campaigns and about organized conflict in general. Thus was born the most famous and influential book on the nature and uses of military violence ever written, *On War.*

The work was not Prussian in either spirit or details: there was nothing limited about Clausewitz's conception of war and not very much that was progressive. His emphasis on absolute victory, to be achieved by physically destroying an opponent's armed forces in battles of annihilation, would have pleased not only Napoleon but Machiavelli and the generals of ancient Rome as well; it would, however, have horrified Frederick the Great. Starting from the oft-quoted premise that "war is nothing other than the continuation of state policy by different means," Clausewitz further maintained that war was "an act of violence intended to compel our opponent to fulfill our will"—an ambiguous statement, to say the least, and one with potentially sinister implications. "War is an act of violence pushed to its utmost bounds," he gushed on, never recognizing that this statement could be used as a rationalization for almost any wartime excess. Echoing Machiavelli specifically, he asserted, "We do not like to hear of generals who are victorious without the shedding of blood." Given the essential nature of armed conflict, he elaborated, it made no sense to try to mitigate it with any "principle of moderation." He had little use for the concept of limited war as developed in the eighteenth century: Clausewitz was a passionate child of Romanticism, not the Enlightenment, and with typical Romantic abandon and disdain for half measures he advised that "the destruction of the enemy's armed force appears . . . always as the superior and more effectual means to which all others must give way."

These themes were destined to be repeated through-out the next century and a half as rationalizations for un-told wartime outrages. Referring to Clausewitz eventually became, for many soldiers, akin to quoting the Bible, though Clausewitz's statements were taken with perhaps even greater literalness. Yet *On War,* like the Bible, had an historical context that made later literal interpretation dangerous. Clausewitz had been writing in direct response to the engulfing nightmare of the Napoleonic Wars, and his work is based on the assumption that war would never be fought in any other way again. Such was untrue, of course: the fact that Napoleon had subordinated every interest of the French nation and people—as well as of those nations and peoples he conquered—to the prosecution of war did not mean that every national leader in the future would do the same. But Clausewitz's fascination with the French emperor—whom he called "the god of war"—was complete, and it blinded him to all other realities and possibilities. His phrases were often elegantly turned and full of conviction; and they became the rallying point for all those who believed that "absolute war" should become the norm. To assert anything else, such people claimed, was to deny the essentially destructive nature of war, to fatuously argue over the niceties of something that in reality had none.

Yet, as J.F.C. Fuller noted, Clausewitz's conception of war was fatally flawed, as was Napoleon's, by a consuming passion for war itself. The young Prussian, Fuller correctly observed, "never grasped that the true aim of war is peace and not victory." In addition, there was one vitally important aspect of war that Clausewitz, while he could not fail to acknowledge it, did his best to gloss over. War had three specific aims, as the supposed military prophet saw it: "(a) To conquer and [not *or*] destroy the enemy's armed force. (b) To get possession of the [enemy's] mate-

rial elements of aggression. . . . (c) To gain public opinion." The first two of these goals could be made to dove-
tail nicely together within Clausewitz's theories; the third
was a very tough fit. Utter destruction of armies and the
seizing of the wide range of infrastructures that support
them, especially in the modern world, do not tend to
make for popularity. Clausewitz's entire work came to be
read as a call for warfare unlimited enough to encompass
deliberate campaigns against all those "elements" in a nation, human and otherwise, that enabled an army to remain in the field—how could he seriously suggest that
such a program would "gain public opinion"? Was there
some way to mesh total conquest with the capture of
enemy hearts and minds?

Clausewitz asserted that there was, but in specifying it
he further revealed the elaborate game of psychological
projection he was playing. Public opinion could be secured, he wrote, only through "great victories" and the
"possession of the enemy's capital." In other words, the
world was populated by people like himself, people who
would be so enraptured and dazzled (or at the very least
demoralized) by the military prowess of a great commander, even if he was an enemy, that they would be rec-
onciled to conquest. That history offered few if any
examples to support this conclusion—that Clausewitz
himself had battled against the object of his admiration
until the latter's final defeat—was neither here nor there.

Destruction, possession, conquest, greatness: these would subdue populations.

We will never know how much gratuitous bloodshed might have been avoided had the brilliantly phrased but no less neurotic and incendiary intellectual exercise that is *On War* slipped quietly into obscurity. But the book was taken up by generations of soldiers and teachers anxious to rationalize unlimited war, and fed in partially as well as wholly digested form to countless military students around the world: this, despite the fact that the principles it espoused were disproved relatively soon after the book's publication by another officer in the Prussian army: Helmuth von Moltke, creator of the modern general-staff system and architect of the three wars (against Denmark in 1864, Austria in 1866, and France in 1870–1871) that were to transform Prussia into modern Germany. A reticent liberal humanist who wrote novels and translated Gibbon, Moltke accepted Clausewitz's maxim that war was an instrument of policy, but he firmly refuted the contention that it therefore needed to be universally destructive in its method and unlimited in its goals; and Moltke backed up his contention with the most progressive campaigns of the nineteenth century.

Moltke's wars offered practical proof that the methods of modern popular and industrial war—which he understood better than any general of his century—were not necessarily inconsistent with Frederick the Great's principle that wars should be fought for specific and limited political objectives. In the opinion of Moltke and his political partner, Prussian chancellor Otto von Bismarck, it was not necessary that these limited objectives be material: Moltke and Bismarck were enough creatures of their time to believe that they were fighting, as Moltke said of the Austrian war, "for an ideal end." But Moltke qualified that end, not as the annexation of territory but rather "the establishment of power," meaning that Austria "had to renounce all part in the hegemony of Germany." He did not talk of "destroying" his enemies, in some vague and overwhelming sense, though he was fully capable of maneuvering them into battles that were renownedly decisive. Possessed of an even more profound and expansive intellect than Clausewitz and unconfused by idolization of Napoleon, Moltke did indeed understand that peace, not devastation, was the purpose of war. It was at least partially due to his influence that the new German state created by Bismarck in 1871 did not use its military primacy to advance its interests on the Continent past the point that other powers could live with.

But farther from home the Clausewitzian ideal of absolute war would be achieved more quickly, by a nation prepared to commit destruction on a level of which even Clausewitz's French idol had likely never dreamed. *On War* was not translated into English until 1873, and it is unlikely that any officer destined to play an important role in the American Civil War ever encountered the German edition of the book. Yet the American martial character had long been moving toward its own promulgation of total or absolute war. Decades of dismal, hard campaigning against Indian tribes following the attainment of independence had deepened the established American inclination toward unconditional resolutions of military contests, an inclination that was thoroughly consistent with the idea of total war. But perhaps nothing had confirmed the belief of many American officers that their nation's enemies must be ruthlessly crushed than a series of memorable events that had occurred in the new capital city of Washington relatively early in the nineteenth century.

In 1814, the United States was engaged in a bitter war, on land and at sea, with its former parent empire, Great Britain. Many analysts of the War of 1812 have tried to explain it as an economic and political conflict of limited importance, but it would have been hard to convince the American civilians who suffered what amounted to terrorist attacks by ruthless British raiding forces that the conflict was either explicable or limited. The British assaults were astoundingly savage: women and children were mutilated and murdered along with civilian men and soldiers in a deliberate attempt to break the American people's will to fight. These efforts reached their culmination in the last days of August 1814, when a squadron of

British ships loaded with soldiers and sailors sailed into Chesapeake Bay and up the Patuxent River with a terrifying objective: to burn the city of Washington to the ground.

The British force succeeded in this goal: by the night of August 24, the White House, the Capitol, the Library of Congress, and many other buildings emblematic of both the newborn capital city and the infant country were engulfed in flames. The government had been evacuated at the last minute, its officers (including President James Madison) scattering across the countryside; but British action against remaining American soldiers and civilians continued to be, in many cases, merciless.

In truth, the War of 1812 had little to do with specific political grievances or economic rivalries: it was prosecuted by the British (who would remain troublesome enemies of the United States throughout the nineteenth century) because of a deep anxiety over the spread of American democratic republicanism. Having seen the bloody anarchy that had overtaken France during its revolution (a revolution at least partially inspired by the American example), and having watched the United States peacefully and dramatically multiply the size of its territory through the Louisiana Purchase, the British empire—a stratified society over which the aristocratic and royal elites had regained significant control following the reestablishment of the constitutional monarchy after

Cromwell's death—had grown fearful that the spread of American-style democratic rebellion would mean not only economic competition abroad but uprisings at home. Thus, the British gratuitously destroyed important structures during the Washington campaign (and killed many innocent people) because those buildings were obnoxious symbols of American values whose spread and propagation the British government feared would spell the disempowerment of its own. As had been the case since long before the Roman era, and as would remain the case, a conflict of larger cultural values proved an even quicker road to a war of terror than a clash of specific political policies or ambitions.

The British were right to fear the encroachment of American democratic republicanism; for in time the rise of the United States did set the example for populations in colonies around the world to seize their own destinies and put an end to the politically and socially regimented system on which such imperial power as Britain's depended. But the tactics that the British army and navy in North America had engaged in to combat these values had opened the empire to the deepest moral criticism, particularly from its longtime nemesis: "How could a nation eminently civilized," asked the *Journal de Paris,* "conduct itself at Washington with as much barbarity as the old banditti of Attila and Genseric? Is not this act of atrocious vengeance a crime against all humanity?"

Crime against humanity or no, the burning of Washington, taken in conjunction with the ongoing Indian wars, was futher proof to many American politicians and military men that notions of limited war had no place on their continent. Few things better exemplified this mentality than the fact that the most powerful and celebrated president between Thomas Jefferson and Abraham Lincoln was Andrew Jackson, who as a boy had witnessed and suffered British cruelties during the revolution, then gone on to make a name for himself as the victor of the final battle of the War of 1812 and as an Indian fighter of uncompromising ferocity. (Jackson's attitude toward Indian tribes would change little during his long presidency.) Americans continued to see themselves, during the first half of the nineteenth century, as a people struggling for survival against enemies who would give no quarter; such being the case, they rarely gave any themselves.

The immediate cause of the American Civil War was similarly influenced by the fruits of American involvement in bitter warfare against civilians, though this exposure had taken place long ago and across the ocean. The African slave trade, as has been said, would not have been possible without the intertribal rivalries and wars that were a constant fact of African life. While the presence of European and American traders willing to purchase human beings undoubtedly exacerbated the drive of many tribes to supply such captives, whites were not inventing a tradition so much as capitalizing on one. (Indeed, the tradition survives to this day, for human slavery remains a valued tribal tradition in certain corners of Africa.) But whatever the exact nature of their complicity in the wars of the African continent, American whites—whether the captains and crews of New England slave ships or the southern farmers who bought their wares—*were* complicit; and though by the time of the Civil War the international slave trade itself was illegal, breeding, owning, or working slaves was not. The economy of the southern states was dependent on the practice, so much so that when the expansion of slavery into new territories was threatened, those states elected to leave the Union. Try as they did, the two sides could find no permanent compromise, for the simple reason that no permanent compromise existed: as even many southerners observed, either slavery and the theories of racial inferiority that underlay it were utterly right (and the northern objections to them utterly wrong), or the southern way of life was founded on lies. Another war of cultural values—this one far more monumental than that of 1812—was in the making in North America; the tactics of terror were close at hand.

Slavery itself may or may not have been, strictly speaking, one such tactic: it *was* the residual result of warfare against civilians waged half a world away, yet it would be difficult to say that the motive of the aggressors in those wars was to politically undercut the tribal governments from which the slaves were taken. But it is beyond doubt that the argument over slavery's continued practice in a country originally inspired by and dedicated to principles of universal freedom unleashed a war that, though a civil conflict, was to have enormous consequences for how greatly terror would characterize international warfare in the future. Certainly, the American government had always proved more than willing to unleash terrorist tactics in its wars with Indian nations, as had the Indians themselves. But would white men turn those tactics against one another, thereby giving the first significant form in the Western world to Clausewitz's vision of a war between modern states in which all elements of society participated in (and were victimized by) the conflict?

The answer was an unequivocal, savage yes, and it was announced even before the war began. Jefferson Davis, a U.S. senator soon to become president of the Confederate States, warned his northern colleagues that they faced the danger of seeing their cities burned and their industrial economy ruined: "The torch and sword can do their work with dreadful havoc, and starving millions would weep at the stupidity of those who had precipitated them into so sad a policy." Many of the generals under Davis's command—particularly Thomas "Stonewall" Jackson, Nathan Bedford Forrest, and Jubal Early—acted on

Davis's threat from early in the war until its final days. Though they rarely had the chance to invade northern territory and never burned a significant northern city, they were able to focus their all-encompassing savagery on not only border towns and farms but Union prisoners of war and former slaves who had been freed to fight against the Confederacy. True, senior commanders such as Robert E. Lee tried to limit such depredations; but in an unbridled war that saw enormous, passionate armies moving through expansive theaters of operations without (especially in the case of the Confederacy) adequate staff systems to ensure compliance with orders of battle, much less discipline, such gentlemanly, limited principles as Lee's were generally ignored—indeed, they were viewed by many as foolish.

The American Civil War, fought with the fantastically destructive weapons of the Industrial Revolution and according to all-engulfing ideas of which not only Karl von Clausewitz but exponents of military terror since the days of the Roman empire would have approved, was a conflict unlike anything the world had ever seen. The Napoleonic Wars had, to be sure, approached it in scope, but the destruction of civilian life and property had not been as systematically, even scientifically, calculated and planned as it was in America. The generals of the south, while they had a true passion and talent for total war, did not have the temperament or the resources to effect such systemization with thorough competence. That task would be performed by the less flamboyant but far more inventive generals of the north and by one in particular: William Tecumseh Sherman.

Often dubbed the "father" and the "philosopher" of total war, Sherman was in fact both—and neither. For at the same time that he recognized, during his army's famously destructive march from Atlanta to the sea and then north through the Carolinas in 1864–1865, that he was breaking the back of the Confederate cause by depriving its armies in the field of weapons and supplies, he also knew that the greater portion of his men's destruction and looting was militarily useless, resembling nothing so much as a Roman punitive raid. The frenetic, brilliant Ohioan made his views known to anyone willing to listen, including the enemy: writing to various city leaders in Atlanta while he was besieging it, Sherman declared, "You cannot qualify war in harsher terms than I will. War is cruelty, and you cannot refine it; and those who brought war into our country deserve all the cruelties and maledictions a people can pour out. . . . You might as well appeal against the thunderstorm as against these terrible hardships of war." At another moment, Sherman declared that he believed himself to be at war with every man, woman, and child in the south; and though he gave orders against excessive foraging, he made little effort to enforce them. "I shall then feel justified in resorting to the harshest measures," he said, in reaction to the resistance and intransigence of the southern people and troops, "and shall make little effort to restrain my army."

The message had, of course, enormous appeal to Union troops who had been fighting a brutal war under mostly incompetent generals for nearly four years. Its effect on the northern public was, by and large, the same. But Sherman's fabled March to the Sea had a much more important and purely military dimension that did not evoke quite so many pseudobiblical declamations from its mastermind but that nonetheless established the march as the most brilliantly conceived and executed single campaign in all of American military history. In its essential character, this military aspect of the march could not have been more at odds with the campaign's darker, punitive dimension: for, judged purely in terms of effect, Sherman's great sweep through the south was limited, progressive warfare at its best. Having learned from long years of attrition to avoid cataclysmic, indecisive battles of annihilation, Sherman focused after the fall of Atlanta on moving through the countryside behind enemy lines, destroying the railways, roads, bridges, and telegraph wires that were the major arteries of supply and communication for the southern forces in the field, especially those farther north, facing Ulysses Grant. Strategically, it was a campaign aimed at victory, not destruction, and there was every possibility that, had gratuitous destruction been avoided, it could have achieved something even greater than victory: meaningful peace. But that troublesome, militarily self-defeating, punitive dimension was not only present, it was emphasized, and its long-term effect was the creation of endless resentment and hatred among the defeated people of the south, who subsequently vented their murderous rage through such homegrown terrorist groups as the Ku Klux Klan. And these groups did not direct their violence against federal troops but against victims over whom they had much more physical and political power: those blacks who were left behind when the federal army went home.

Sherman was among the most compulsively loquacious of men, yet we may never truly know why he gave in so completely to an impulse that he openly recognized as unnecessary. So aware was he, in fact, of exactly how much of his army's destruction was important to hastening the surrender of the south and how much was not that he (typically) worked out a precise ratio. In Georgia alone, he said, his army did one hundred million dollars' worth of damage; of that, only twenty million "inured to our advantage." As for the rest, it was "simple waste and destruction." Yet it was not, in fact, so simple; not when we factor in the harm it did to the cause, not of winning the war but of winning the peace. Certainly, the Confederacy was defeated, even before Sherman could complete the last phase of his campaign. (Given its long history of indulging in terror, the Confederacy was unlikely to have suffered any other fate.) But while defeated, the south was also, due to Union brutality, laced with lingering resentment and brutality. In other words, the long-term interests of the American nation—which, as stated by Lincoln, were to pacify the south and heal internal divisions—suffered seriously because of that useless 80 percent of damage done by Sherman's army. The tactics of retaliatory terror—in this case, inflicting starvation, murder, and destruction as payment for not only starting the war but maintaining a vicious system of human slavery—proved as self-defeating in America as they had anywhere else in the world. The war would have been won without them; the peace was lost because of them.

On many occasions, Sherman protested that he was simply incapable of controlling the vengeful impulses of his men; but this seems wholly disingenuous when one considers the immense force of his character, or when placed against his even more numerous statements of his intention—his *choice*—to "make the old and young, rich and poor, feel the hard hand of war." Rarely has a commander and a campaign been at once so brilliant and so misguided. Of course, Sherman's vengeful pronouncements *did* fit into the uncompromising tradition that characterized the American style of war, as did all the other gratuitous destruction perpetrated by Civil War generals, to say nothing of the north's ultimate demand for unconditional surrender from the south. In this continuity lies another cause for disappointment at Sherman's actions and words: the vast majority of American commanders who came after him would remember not the brilliant progressive side of his southern campaign but the vengefully destructive dimension. America's military tradition was already weighted in favor of using massed forces to utterly devastate an enemy; the destructive behavior of nearly all its armies during the Civil War ensured that this tradition would live on and gather strength.

Thus many foreign observers, looking at the United States at the time of the Civil War, did not see a nation valiantly struggling for freedom and liberty. Rather, they quite understandably saw a people bringing the terrifying Clausewitzian vision of war to life. This perception was only reinforced when, following the Civil War, American commanders—led by Sherman himself—turned their attention to subduing the remaining North American Indian tribes once and for all. The tenor of those wars was bluntly summed up by General Philip Sheridan (another of the Union army's masters of gratuitous destruction) when he famously remarked, "The only good Indians I ever saw were dead." The campaigns that took place in the American West during the final quarter of the nineteenth century endure to this day as examples that any repressive government or murderous group can use to argue against American moral validity; and thus they must finally be considered eminently self-defeating. These were true wars of terror, campaigns of extermination and annihilation in which treaties were broken, noncombatants were not only legitimate but prime targets, and no weapons (not even, reportedly, blankets laced with smallpox) were placed beyond consideration by the American government or its often shadowy agents—all facts that are chillingly pertinent to our current situation.

When Prussia's Helmuth von Moltke turned his considerable mental powers to studying the American Civil War, he could find little that he deemed of value, and he finally dubbed the struggle a mere clash of armed mobs. Yet events on his continent—indeed, within his own country—soon began to show their own signs of Clausewitzian trouble. During the Franco-Prussian War of 1870–1871—a conflict that, thanks to Moltke's innovative planning and shrewd exploitation of modern technology, could not have stood in more contrast to the American Civil War—Chancellor Bismarck decided, once the Prussian army had surrounded Paris and effectively won the contest, that it was necessary to "possess" the French capital. The best way to bring about this possession, he believed, was a strong dose of long-range artillery bombardment that would break the Parisians' spirits. Moltke fervently opposed the idea on the grounds that the city, by then, was of no military value and contained almost nothing but civilians. Nor would it simply be immoral to bombard them, Moltke protested; it would also be counterproductive, as it was likely to stiffen rather than weaken French resistance. Moltke's opinion was the result of a lifetime's careful study of military history; but Bismarck was chancellor, and the city was shelled. True to Moltke's predictions, the roar of the guns brought tougher opposition, and, more important for the future of Europe, French bitterness toward Germany was increased and prolonged dramatically.

With the conclusion of the Franco-Prussian War, however, Europe entered into several decades of general peace and prosperity. Yet the chief of the German general staff had seen something in both the American Civil War and the bombardment of Paris that disturbed him so profoundly that he worked for the rest of his life to make sure that Germany did not enter another war. The conflicts of the future, Moltke feared, would resemble not those that he had orchestrated but rather the variety that Clausewitz had called for, that the Americans had fought, and that Bismarck had advocated outside Paris. In 1890, just a year before his death, Moltke used his seat in the upper house of the German Reichstag to voice his anxieties in a speech to which almost no one paid serious attention.

Europe, he said, had been in danger of a general war for nearly a decade, despite its great prosperity. Given the rising economic and colonial competition among the powers, there seemed little reason to think that this conflict could be put off forever. When it finally did come, there would be no way to predict how long it might last: "Gentlemen," warned the master of progressive nineteenth-century warfare, "it may be a seven-year, it may be a thirty-year war—and woe to him who sets fire to Europe, who first puts the flame to the powderkeg!"

Despite his advanced age, Moltke had very realistic suspicions about who that guilty party would turn out to be. But whoever started the next war, Moltke remained certain until the day he died that it would be unrestrained in its passions, total in its scope, and horrendous in its nature. The entire world stood on the verge of a new century and a new way of life, one that might well feature the triumph of those who believed that war was unreformable and unrestrainable—in other words, one that might be dominated, rather than merely visited, by terror.

CHAPTER EIGHT

FASCINATED BY TERROR

The nineteenth century witnessed an outbreak of scattered international political violence that is interpreted by many today as the historical precedent from which we should derive our approach to modern terrorism. The agents of this violence, commonly lumped together as "anarchists," ostensibly used individual murders and assassinations, as well as bombings of military units, law-enforcement officers, and private industrial-security forces, as methods of both calling attention to and battling the increasing disparities in wealth and living standards among economic classes that were a result of the ongoing Industrial Revolution. The anarchists' ultimate goal was to precipitate a full-scale international workers' uprising and beyond that to destroy the oppression of government by ending government itself. Following the teachings of Mikhail Bakunin, Pyotr Kropotkin, Sergei

Nechayev, and others, anarchists spread fear not only among the wealthy in Europe and America but also among average citizens, who often made up the collateral damage of what became a heated, long-running battle throughout the Western world.

As in the case of guerrilla war, there are unquestionable similarities between anarchism and modern-day terrorism; indeed, the word *terrorist* became a term of common usage in response to the anarchist threat. The overall anarchist message was a vague and unattainable one—"We object to all legislation, all authority, and all influence . . . ," said Bakunin, "even when it is based on universal suffrage"—just as are most terrorist rants; and anarchism's central aim, again like that of terrorism, was to create an atmosphere of fear and instability that would weaken the loyalty of the average citizen to his or her government. Anarchist weapons of choice were as rudimentary as are those of many terrorists—knives, pistols, and homemade bombs—and they did not shy away from suicide attacks. In one famous incident in 1892, Alexander Berkman, an anarchist of Russian origins working in America, stormed the office of industrialist Henry Clay Frick (who had handled the infamous Homestead strike for his boss, Andrew Carnegie), shot Frick in the neck and stabbed at his legs (Frick lived), and finally, while being subdued by police and detectives, tried to ignite an explosive capsule with his teeth. Other anarchist killers

were far more successful than Berkman, murdering busi-
nessmen, statesmen, and aristocrats—even a tsar of Russia, a king of Italy, and, in 1901, the American president,
William McKinley—with such regularity that the United
States passed laws that forbade anyone with known anarchist connections from entering the country. But there
were already more than enough anarchists in America to
do a great deal of harm, as evidenced by McKinley's death
at the hands of Leon Czolgosz, a creature so unbalanced
that even many anarchist groups had been reluctant to
allow him into their ranks.

Violent as it was, the anarchist movement never represented a truly significant threat either to established business interests or to the stability of Western governments.
And it is precisely this absence of serious threat that
makes so many political and historical analysts anxious to
view them as the precursors to modern international terrorists: if terrorists are no more than a new generation of
anarchists, their threat is much more limited. But today's
terrorists have many strengths that the anarchists did not.
First and foremost, the anarchists had no state sponsors,
which meant that they had no paramilitary training facilities (which they certainly could have used, since they
tended to be half-starved intellectuals with little or no
practical experience of violence), as well as no extensive
intelligence systems and no access to the most up-to-date
military weapons. (Their occasional use of more primi-

tive arms notwithstanding, most terrorists can indeed handle sophisticated military hardware.) In terms of organization, too, although anarchists often worked in cells, they lacked the advanced technical skills and equipment necessary for effective encryption and protected communication. The cells could be infiltrated and exposed without the difficulty that international law-enforcement agencies and intelligence services experience when tracking today's terrorists, who have demonstrated a sound working knowledge of all levels of communications and information technology.

In short, there was never any point at which the anarchist movement represented the kind of genuine paramilitary or military threat that contemporary terrorists now pose; and the terrorist movement has not achieved that threat potential by emulating the tactics of anarchism or any other fringe group. Rather, they have adopted the military model of their enemies, training according to rigorous programs in dedicated facilities built in sponsor states with the support of often wealthy backers. Much as it may soothe many people's nerves to think that a terrorist bomb is effectively indistinguishable from an anarchist bomb, the two weapons are made radically different by their designers' and users' different training and goals. For all their posturing, anarchists effectively *were* criminals, and as such were most effectively pursued using the methods that we have been accustomed to using against terrorists: those of law enforcement. In a complementary irony, it is modern terrorists who have achieved the anarchist dream of becoming an international army of enormous destructive potential. Thus we are led back to the history of warfare, rather than to that of political extremism, in our effort to determine how best to respond to the terrorist threat.

Although there exists no truly meaningful similarity between past anarchists and present terrorists, there *is* such a similarity among their enemies. The modern form of multinational corporate capitalism that travels in tandem with Western cultural expansionism has given fuel to the fury of many international terrorists by creating the impression that any and all regional concerns are subordinate to the interests of Western businesses. Further, it is a direct, if more benign, outgrowth of the imperial breed of capitalism that dominated the West at the turn of the last century. Corporate officers of today deny this, of course, feigning indignation and shock that their methods of doing business are viewed by some as little more than imperialism without the political regalia. Yet the concerns of international commerce in 1900 were strikingly similar to those in 2000: questions of international tariff rates and trade wars, of the impact of immigration, of the encroaching influence of Western goods and cultures in less developed countries, of how to regulate (or avoid the regulation of) the exploitation of global natural resources, even of how to open the Chinese market to greater economic penetration—all these were pressing issues a hundred years ago. The real difference between the international economies of now and then is that the West in 1900 displayed little hesitation in using troops to impose its commercial will around the world.

Of course, many observers say that the West displays precious little hesitation about using its military might to protect corporate interests *now;* and while there is an unquestionable discrepancy between the two periods in terms of the frequency and scale of such use, an undeniable similarity of its purpose and effect sometimes exists. (Few people still maintain, for example, that the Gulf War was solely or even primarily undertaken to liberate Kuwait; it resembles a nineteenth-century war to protect overseas commercial interests far more than it does, say, the invasion of France in 1944.) The principal domestic effect of such action, for Western nations, was and remains cost—not to business but to citizens. While most people today are aware that forceful efforts by Western governments to protect democratic capitalist values and the interests of multinational corporations overseas place an enormous burden on the taxpayers of their home nations, many are surprised to discover that an identical situation prevailed during the age of de facto political imperialism a century ago. The possession and administration of colonies was never a particularly profitable business for, say, Britain or France. It was spectacularly profitable for those British or French businesses that gained access to such colonies, but the annual return to national governments themselves never exceeded, by most estimates, some 3 to 5 percent. This does not, however, validate the traditional leftist view that Western governments were acting in the knowing, paid service of international business during the age of imperialism. Most imperialist statesmen of true stature—including Americans such as Theodore Roosevelt, who pushed hard for the annexation of the Philippines after the American war with Spain in 1898—genuinely believed that they were performing a moral service by bringing Western liberal democracy to the world. The "white man's burden," a phrase met with derision and scorn today, was at the time a genuine, if in many cases misguided, sentiment, and it powered turn-of-the-century imperialism to a very significant extent.

Western culture in the nineteenth century, in other words, came into contact with many new and distant parts of the globe in much the same way that Islamic evangelism had more than a millennium earlier: convinced that the world wanted the material and spiritual advantages it had to offer and prepared to impose those advantages forcefully, if need be. This, of course, meant war; and war, in the West of the nineteenth century, meant *total* war. Yet, perhaps surprisingly, this martial concept was far easier for many indigenous people to accept and integrate than were such things as Christianity or steam engines. For while industrial goods and notions of a single god may have been new and shocking to many such people, unlimited war was not. As we have seen, for generations such conflict had been the rule on battlefields in almost every part of the world *except* the West, and during the nineteenth century the situation only intensified. Perhaps the greatest example of the dominance of unlimited war during this period was the Taiping Rebellion in China, during which the Manchu dynasty, now corrupt and ailing, and a group of quasi-Christian fanatics battled for better than a decade, killing upward of forty million people.

The only things lacking in such conflicts were large numbers of up-to-date weapons: Western rifles, muskets, and artillery were prized rarities in most parts of the world. During the Taiping Rebellion, for example, the overwhelming majority of the forty million who died perished by sword, spear, torture, or starvation. One can only wonder how much higher the casualty figures would have been had the rifled arms and high explosives available in Europe and America at the time been a significant factor in the contest. All too soon, however, thanks not only to the dramatic expansion of trade (and concurrent slackening of ethics) brought about by nineteenth-century imperial capitalism but also to the advances in techniques of mass production on which that capitalism depended, such weapons would indeed be available to any country, faction, or individual who had the money to pay for them. In fact, the companies that manufactured such arms were soon producing them so quickly that they required large numbers of new customers, and a burgeoning international arms trade grew out of the healthy one that already existed.

In short, what had been the single most terrible aspect of the American Civil War—large-scale butchery made possible by weapons that were far more advanced than the minds of the men using them—showed, by the end of the century, every sign of spreading into the farthest corners of the globe. When combined with the fact that anti-Western and anti-imperialist movements were sprouting up with increasing regularity in those far corners, the destructive potential of this trend was magnified dramatically.

The British repeatedly experienced the dangerously effective levels at which indigenous populations in colonies and prospective colonies were capable of fighting during the nineteenth century; and their tutoring came, for the most part, from Muslim armies in former provinces of the now-disintegrating Ottoman empire. First and foremost, and of greatest relevance to our current terrorist

war, was the question of Afghanistan, a khanate that became a British obsession at mid-century. It was through
Afghanistan, the British were convinced, that Russia
would threaten India, the "jewel in the crown" of the
British empire and a primary source of raw materials and
trade for British business. Three times—from 1839 to
1842, in 1878, and again in 1879—the British went to
war in Afghanistan to forestall Russian designs. The problem was that they fought not Russians but Afghans who
were supposedly sympathetic to the Russians, or who
were simply fiercely independent, which the British regarded as equally dangerous. Such actions eventually
turned even pro-British Afghans against them: indeed,
the third Afghan war was prompted by a mutiny on the
part of supposedly loyal Afghan troops, who massacred
the head of the British mission in Kabul and his entire
staff. The British had not been prepared for how much
the Afghans resented being pawns in what came to be
called the "great game" of central Asian diplomacy: well
armed and determined, they became one of the most continuous demonstrations of the limits of British imperial
ambitions.

Africa, too, had ugly surprises in store for the British.
In 1879, with their attention focused on Afghanistan, the
leaders of the empire received the shocking news that a
significant British military force had been massacred in

South Africa by a Zulu army that as yet was fighting with little more than spears. The Zulus soon learned the use of more modern arms captured from the British, but a worse problem was also developing farther north, in the Sudan.

There, a fundamentalist Muslim movement sprang up under the leadership of one Muhammad Ahmad, who claimed to be "the Mahdi," a mythic, neomessianic figure in Islamic lore. Acting in defiance of their corrupt, ineffectual Egyptian and Ottoman masters, as well as of the London government that had long been propping up both the Cairo and Constantinople regimes, the Mahdi's followers defeated an Egyptian army commanded by a British mercenary, capturing and learning the use of their weapons. These they used to attack the remaining Egyptians and loyal Sudanese, who had rallied around another British general, Charles "Chinese" Gordon, a national hero in Britain and a favorite of Queen Victoria's. Gordon masterminded a brilliant defense of the Sudanese capital of Khartoum but was eventually overrun and killed in 1885; for the next fourteen years, the Mahdist regime (the Mahdi himself died soon after Gordon) posed a worrisome threat to London's interests in the region. The movement was eventually quelled with stunning, high-tech brutality by Britain's General Herbert Kitchener, who ordered his troops to make liberal use of the Maxim gun, an extremely effective, carriage-mounted machine gun that cut the Muslims down in droves. As one British war correspondent wrote of the encounter, "It was not a battle but an execution."

In the Philippines, meanwhile, the United States entered into a similarly horrifying war with those Filipinos who had been foolish enough to think that the Americans, having liberated them from Spanish rule, would next grant them their independence. American troops instead subdued the nationalist guerrillas in a war that involved the widespread targeting and abuse of civilians by both sides. The war was undertaken in part because the ordinarily isolationist William McKinley felt a sense of responsibility to "lift up" what he saw as the savage Filipinos. While this sentiment was sincere (if terribly naïve), it was also exploited by those in- and outside the government who desperately desired a naval base from which the United States could assert its "prestige"—specifically its claim to a share of the China trade. Anti-imperialists in America decried the war, and a significant antiwar movement broke out. The vast majority of Americans, however, had grown accustomed to reports of such bitter conflicts through the Indian wars in their own Western states and territories, which did not reach their effective end until just before the Philippine campaign began. Largely because of this general inurement—and also because most Americans did not know, in the words of newspaper humorist Finley P. Dunne, whether the Philippines "were islands or canned goods"—moral outrage in America never truly coalesced, and the archipelago was kept.

In the middle of the century, France had received its share of humiliation in Algeria from the legendary Abd al-Kader, whose desert exploits led French troops to engage in "scorched earth" tactics against local communities that were as "absolute" as anything of which Karl von Clausewitz had ever dreamed, as well as on a par with anything William Tecumseh Sherman would ever achieve: Alexis de Tocqueville, after visiting Algeria in 1846, claimed that the savage nature of the war there was turning French soldiers into bloodthirsty brutes. France eventually prevailed, but, again, terror bought success in the short run, disaster in the long: Algeria was to remain a trouble spot for the French for generations, and indeed today it is a home to, and training ground for, some of the world's most dangerous terrorists.

In all of these conflicts, Westerners were repeatedly threatened and actually killed by natives in their domestic employ or serving (as in the case of the Afghan mutiny of 1879) in their armed forces—the same imperial problem that had proved so thorny for the Romans. What was perhaps most remarkable about these phenomena was not that they occurred, and not even that they were so indiscriminate in their violence (again, total war was nothing new to most of the non-Western world); rather, it was the fact that the colonial powers were so often caught off guard by them, seeming never to truly learn from experience. But the plain fact was that imperialism depended on native levies and volunteers to function: there simply were not enough Western troops to patrol the whole of their colonized territories, and so deals had to be struck with certain indigenous elements, some of which could be trusted, most of which were simply biding their time, gaining weapons and training as they waited for an opportunity to eject what they perceived as invaders.

The list of so-called imperial wars that were total in scope was not confined to those that pitted Westerners against indigenous peoples. The Boer War of 1899–1902, for example, saw the British empire fighting against transplanted European settlers of primarily Dutch extraction, in a conflict characterized on both sides by the open abuse and murder of civilians and prisoners. Indeed, so bitter did the war become that the British, taking a leaf from the book of a notoriously brutal Spanish military administrator of Cuba prior to the Spanish-American War, built "concentration camps" for the Boers. These British camps were the brainchild of the same General Kitchener who had earlier taken such delight in turning his Maxim guns on Sudanese warriors, as well as on their women and children. Further evidence of Kitchener's unique psychological qualifications for modern warfare had been offered at the conclusion of the Sudanese campaign, when he had exhumed the Mahdi's body and destroyed everything save the skull, his intention being to make a drinking cup or an inkstand out of the thing. More sensitive and sensible souls had prevailed on Kitchener to allow the skull to be reinterred; yet this was the man who would later be selected to be Britain's secretary of state for war at the outbreak of the Great War.

Many volumes have been expended in the cause of determining how the European cataclysm of 1914–1918—a war that, like the American Civil War, was not expected to be a long one by the men who planned it—could have ended up being so interminable and so unrestrainedly savage. When placed in the context of global military development and activity in the years leading up to it, however, the war's brutal nature is really not surprising at all. Herbert Kitchener was not the only senior European military officer who had learned the ways of total war abroad; nor was it only the military departments of the combatant governments that were filled with such veterans. Winston Churchill, for example, who served as Britain's first lord of the Admiralty at the start of the 1914–1918 conflict, had, like Kitchener, seen action during the fight against the Boers; and he, too, had learned never to shrink from the brutal demands of total war. The Admiralty was responsible for executing the "Orders in Council," with which Britain rewrote international maritime law to give itself permission to blockade—that is to say, *starve*—not only the German armed forces but the population of Germany generally. And when the Germans attempted to counteract the blockade through the only effective means at their disposal—submarine warfare against merchant shipping—it was Churchill who schemed endlessly to get the submarines to provide some sort of an "incident" that would lead to the entrance of the neutral United States into the war on the Allied side. That eventual incident, of course, was the sinking of the passenger liner *Lusitania*—an event that Churchill could scarcely have done more to facilitate if he had been steering the ship himself.

Both the British blockade of Germany and the German submarine counterstrategy fit entirely within the definition of international terrorism as warfare waged deliberately against civilians in order to weaken those civilians' support for the policies of their government; and both, in the tradition of *many* terrorist campaigns, succeeded in the short term but backfired in the long. Though the British blockade did cost many civilian lives within Germany, those deaths steeled the German public and infuriated German soldiers. The German government, on the other hand, treated the U-boat crew that sank the *Lusitania* as heroes; but when the full weight of American military might descended on the German forces in the field, the cost of that and similar acts of high-seas terror became apparent. Never had there been a clearer demonstration that the line between conventional warfare and the tactic of deliberately attacking and mistreating civilians for political purposes—terrorism—had begun once again to blur in the only part of the world that had ever worked to keep the two concepts apart.

The results of this blurring were dramatic, impressive, and plain to see, even to seemingly remote and unconcerned nations. The map of Europe was not only redrawn macrocosmically, by the gleeful, foolish victors at Versailles, but microcosmically as well. Whole villages and towns had disappeared under the kind of indiscriminate artillery bombardment that Helmuth von Moltke had argued against, and civilian life generally had been assaulted in ways that had not before been technologically feasible. Particularly when the turgidity of most of the strategies and tactics devised by the war's military commanders is also considered, it is difficult not to view the First World War as an exercise in terrorism on the grand scale: from poison gas to mass murder on the high seas, Europeans and Americans broke nearly every code of wartime conduct they had previously established for themselves. Of course, they had committed such breaches against non-Western peoples long before; and being as most of those non-Western peoples had never understood what all the fuss over "rules of war" had been about in the first place,

it can be safely said that the most distressing casualty of
the war, in a very real sense, was the ability of any national, tribal, ethnic, or regional leader in the world to
speak with true credibility on the subject of how to regulate the conduct of international conflict.

Such leaders would continue to try, however. They
repeatedly gathered at Geneva during the 1920s to augment the 1864 and 1906 protocols that had called for
rules regarding medical treatment of combatants, as well
as of medical personnel themselves, and had also determined regulations for maritime war (which the British
had promptly and unilaterally broken in 1914). The new
protocols outlawed the use of chemical and biological
weapons and set out a code for the treatment of prisoners
of war. Yet these treaties had no effective penalty provi-
sions, nor were many of the new states created out of the
ruins of the defeated Central Powers—Germany, Austria-
Hungary, Turkey (or what was left of the Ottoman empire), and Bulgaria—even signatory. And, of course, no
peoples whose lands continued to comprise European
colonies had any voice in such affairs, or any reason or inclination to take such ideas seriously.

But the most significant result of the First World War,
so far as terrorism on the smaller scale of bombings, murder, and political subversion is concerned, was the establishment of the first true national sanctuary for those who

wished to learn such tactics: the first real state sponsor of terrorism. For hundreds of years, the Russian people, most of them living in a perpetual state of medieval feudalism, had been ruled by the peculiar blend of reactionary viciousness and imperial opulence called tsarism. But the war had bankrupted the tsarist system and opened the way to revolution and a new form of violent governmental oppression: Bolshevism. Though it would be rhapsodized by Western leftists as the first true "workers' state," the Soviet Union was in fact a dictatorship, ruled by a comparatively small clique of middle- and lower-middle-class intellectuals and autocrats. Their revered leader, Vladimir Lenin, was a man with a keen appreciation of all types of terrorism, domestic and international: "In principle we have never rejected terror," he admitted frankly, "nor can we reject it." But Lenin also saw where an overreliance on terror would take his new state, warning his comrades that "our duty is to warn most energetically against too much fascination by terror, against regarding it as the main and basic means of struggle, something to which so many are inclined at this time."

The man who would be called the "high priest of terror" was not exaggerating. The number of his followers who had become fascinated by and addicted to terror as a basic governmental policy soon grew so high that they en-

sured, through their repressive violence, that their dynasty would not last the century. Long before it fell,
however—indeed, shortly after its inception—it became
a safe haven where almost anyone with anti-Western and
anticapitalist views could come to be physically and mentally trained, as well as armed to fight both terrorist and
guerrilla campaigns. So great was the fear aroused in
Western capitalist democracies by this and other evidence
of the Soviet desire to export Leninist revolution that they
became enthralled by their own retaliatory form of terror;
and the conflicts and destruction bred by these two com-
peting terrorist styles were to rage on even after the Soviet
state had crumbled under the weight of its own people's
torment.

CHAPTER NINE

THIS FUNDAMENTALLY REPUGNANT PHILOSOPHY

That most quixotic of American sagas, Woodrow Wilson's quest to first structure a League of Nations during the Paris Peace Conference of 1919 and then convince his countrymen to join it, had profound implications for the course and conduct of global conflict during the nightmarish generation that followed. Wilson's criminally narcissistic willingness to sacrifice almost any principle and any cause to his personal holy grail did not simply ensure that Germany would be so brutalized by the terms of peace that it would seek violent redress as soon as it was able; the American president's blind pursuit of political sainthood also meant that a broad array of nations and leaders who had played important roles in the war effort— not least the tribes of the Arabian peninsula that had risen in revolt against one of Germany's principal allies, the Ottoman empire—would have their quests for full-fledged independence complicated and prolonged by a morass of European mandates, protectorates, and spheres of influence, arrangements that were little more than euphemistic covers for the new Western interest in—and eventual lust for—oil. Ultimately, of course, the American Senate made the League of Nations for which Wilson had sold not only his own but millions of other souls at Versailles irrelevant by refusing to compromise American military authority sufficiently to make entrance into the organization possible. But bitterness and frustration had been sown all over the world, ensuring that the Second World War (now generally and correctly seen as nothing more than a continuation of the first) would be even broader in scope than the preceding "war to end all wars."

Wilson's behavior at Versailles was also warped by a presumptive belief about European—specifically German—affairs, one that his British and French allies were only too happy to encourage. Like many of his countrymen, the president was convinced that Europe's ills were largely the result of "Prussianism." The kingdom that had engineered the unification of Germany was, it continued to be widely thought, peopled by a narrow, aggressive, violent race, ever anxious to whip up new conflicts and use the most savage means to win them. This perception had, of course, been the result of German behavior during the First World War alone. The political and military cliques that had surrounded the arrogant, foolish Kaiser Wilhelm

II had proved willing to engage in a strategy (a simultaneous two-front war against France and Russia) and tactics (the use of poison gas and the deliberate murder of civilians, especially in Belgium) that were in no way consistent with the progressive, limited tradition established by the philosopher-king Frederick the Great, a tradition that had weathered the apostate ideas of Karl von Clausewitz and then been reinvigorated during the long military stewardship of the scholar-soldier Helmuth von Moltke. The truth was that Prussia had, over the course of European history, been vastly less guilty of disturbing the general peace of Europe than, say, France, which had rarely let a century or even a generation go by without producing an egomaniacal king or emperor bent on continental hegemony or outright domination. But vengeance, in 1919 as always, was a more powerful human instinct than historical awareness, and so the German army and its primarily Prussian officer corps was stripped down to the barest of bones at Versailles, the Allied negotiators proudly congratulating one another on their humiliation of "the Hun."

The unintended result of this attempted emasculation was, ironically, the last and greatest stand of Prussian-style progressive warfare. After all, Prussia had had its army trimmed by conquerors before—Napoleon had been the last to achieve it—but it had also proved able to work within the restrictions to rise back up and repay the insult. The Prussian officer corps between the two world wars had no similar notions of rising up (that was the dream of a group of Austrian and Bohemian deviants and psychopaths), but they took their oath to safeguard the inflation- and indemnity-racked German state seriously. There was no reason to believe that Germany's former enemies, particularly the French, would not seize the first opportunity to annex German territory or squeeze more penalties out of the already starving German people, particularly after the Great Depression struck. Yet the German officer corps had virtually nothing to work with, militarily: a minuscule army with no advanced weapons, and no air force at all. For such an organization ever to succeed in the field again, it would have to rely even more than it had for the preceding two centuries (with the exception, again, of the anomalous First World War era) on limiting and specifying its political and military aims, achieving surprise through bold, offensively oriented strategies, and avoiding large-scale battles of attrition. Thus the spirit of Frederick the Great was reborn amid the humiliation of Versailles: the Germans devised and pursued a new strategic and tactical concept of which that legendary ruler would have wholly approved, one that they called *blitzkrieg:* "lightning war."

The term has since entered popular use to such an extent that it has lost nearly all its original meaning and importance: for blitzkrieg was, simply put, the height of modern progressive war, the single most successful means for prosecuting an offensive campaign ever devised in the industrial age. The tactic was best summed up by one of its interwar-era British adherents and theorists, England's J.F.C. Fuller: "It was to employ mobility as a psychological weapon: not to kill but to move; not to move to kill but to move to terrify, to bewilder, to perplex, to cause consternation, doubt and confusion in the rear of the enemy, which rumour would magnify until panic became monstrous. In short, its aim was to paralyse not only the enemy's command but also his government, and paralysation would be in direct proportion to velocity."

By realizing the immense potential of two relatively new arms of military service—armored divisions and tactical air squadrons—the German general staff fashioned a compact fighting machine that was enormously maneuverable. And, just as important, they trained an officer corps that, in keeping with another Prussian tradition, read much and widely. The non-German advocates of what would in English come to be called mobile mechanized warfare—men whose books and papers often went unread in their own countries—found eager colleagues and disciples in Germany. The goal of all these thinkers was the same: to avoid, in any future wars, the kind of protracted horror through which they had just lived and fought, and attempt to combine continued advances in industrial technology with established principles of lim-

ited, progressive warfare. It was a combination that
had worked spectacularly well for Moltke in the three
nineteenth-century wars that had established German
military dominance; and it was a combination that would
serve a far more nefarious German regime even better
when the Second World War broke out in 1939.

Unfortunately, the high commands of the First World
War's Allied powers, flush with their victory and dominated by men whose teeth had been cut during the unlimited butchery of colonial and frontier conflicts, were
uninterested in such inventive principles as blitzkrieg.
Fuller's writings, and those of such British colleagues as
Basil Liddell Hart, fell for the most part on deaf ears at
home; the days of Drake and Cromwell were gone and
forgotten. And the situation in America was only worse:
the British did at least produce significant *theorists* of mobile mechanized warfare during the interwar period, as
did the French, in the person of future president Charles
de Gaulle (although de Gaulle was heeded by his government to an only marginally greater extent than his British
counterparts were by theirs). But the Americans—as always uninterested in military advances until war was
thrust upon them—were quite content to rely on the traditions of attrition and total war established by the commanders of the Civil War and the Indian conflicts: when
the Second World War broke out, the American army still
had active horse cavalry units, and tanks were, so far as

most American senior commanders were concerned, little more than self-propelled artillery.

Only in Germany were native theorists of lightning war given their head, and even there the decision was neither unanimous nor confident. Many older officers considered the new strategy and tactics that were being vigorously promoted by men such as Heinz Guderian to be excessively risky, as indeed did the eventual German head of state, Adolf Hitler. And although Hitler was forced by a combination of circumstance and incessant pressure from the blitzkrieg prophets to allow them to test their ideas during the invasion of Poland in 1939, he remained uneasy, even after the German *panzer* (armored) divisions achieved victory in a matter of weeks and with remarkably little cost. Poland, German critics said, was a small, backward country; how would the new form of warfare do when employed against a major power? That answer was provided in France during the spring of 1940, when the German armored divisions and their tactical air-support units achieved even more stunning—and speedy—results than they had in Poland. And yet still Hitler, though jubilant over the victory, was uneasy. There was something about blitzkrieg that simply did not sit well with him, and it is not hard to realize what it was.

Hitler had created, between 1933 and 1940, one of the two most fundamentally terrorist states that the West-

ern world had ever seen (the other being Nazi Germany's
neighbor to the east, the Soviet Union, presided over by
Lenin's successor, Josef Stalin). Destruction on a mass
scale was the essence of the Nazi ethic: destruction of internal "impurities," as well as destruction of external enemies. The entire underlying philosophy of the "new"
Germany was fantastically reactionary, reaching for its inspiration and its attitude toward human life back to the
Dark Ages. Blitzkrieg, on the other hand, though it drew
on the ideas of Frederick the Great and Moltke, was an
utterly modern permutation of their thinking, a completely new way of making war that was aimed not at the
physical destruction but rather the defeat of the enemy.
Furthermore, the idea had been devised by the regular
military, and Hitler distrusted the "Prussians" almost as
much as did the Allies. (Though Hitler, unlike the Allies,
had good grounds for his distrust: the Prussian military
elite was the only group within Germany that, when
forced to acknowledge the genocidal and suicidal terror
that was laced through all of Hitler's schemes, almost succeeded in assassinating him.) Finally, Prussian military
concepts had always rested on the idea of limiting and
specifying goals and ambitions—an attitude that obviously did not serve Hitler's purposes. Certainly, Hitler
made *use* of the army and its new ideas, and the army,
thrilled by the prospect of reasserting German pride,
prostituted itself to a man and a party that they dis-

dained. But Hitler was never truly satisfied with the arrangement, and as soon as he was free to revert to less limited tactics—tactics that would more *totally* embody his taste for terror—he leapt at the chance, or, as it happened, at the pair of chances.

Hitler's first opportunity to deliberately wage war against not an army but a civilian population came with the 1940–1941 air war against Britain. The second was offered by the plan, tested in Poland but not perfected until the 1941 invasion of Russia, to simply murder all conquered citizens that were of no use in Nazi concentration camps or to any other departments of the German forced-labor machine. That Russians, Jews and otherwise, were being slaughtered on the spot or deported in massive numbers was known to every German army officer who served during the eastern campaign, and in this knowledge lies guilt that cannot be erased by ideas concerning progressive warfare or by subsequent attempts to murder Hitler. Such tactics were, as always, counterproductive: the bombing of London and other British cities had an astoundingly galvanizing effect on the British people, as did Germany's extermination campaign on the Russians. But they also instilled, again predictably, an intense desire for revenge, and in acting on that desire—in answering terror with terror—the Allies committed acts that only made their task of winning the war more difficult.

The oxymoronically titled "strategic bombing" campaign carried out by Allied planes throughout the war, particularly during its last years, was officially intended to damage German industrial production, as well as infrastructure that facilitated military operations. But in truth, Allied commanders never seriously doubted that high-altitude bombing of open cities would lead to massive civilian casualties; they simply did not care, or were actively enthusiastic, about the tactic's punitive dimension. Certainly this was the attitude of Prime Minister Winston Churchill, whose sensitivity to the loss of civilian life had only diminished since the First World War: Churchill's stated purpose in continuing the bombing runs was "to make the enemy burn and bleed in every way."

On the most obvious level, this campaign was also self-defeating: it instilled a renewed will to resist in the German army and people, rather than breaking their spirit as had been planned. Indeed, German industrial production actually *increased* as the volume of bombs dropped multiplied, and the range of ages of men and boys who volunteered for service in the army expanded. But even worse, such variations on the standard theme of terrorism established a pattern of military behavior that the nations of the West, and especially the United States, have not been able to break to this day. The central belief that the Germans could be pounded into submission from the air—the same belief that had first possessed European military commanders when long-range cannon became available to them in the late Middle Ages and that had lasted through the siege of Paris in 1871 and on into the static, pummeling madness of the First World War— fit precisely with the American military tradition established during the vast majority of Civil War campaigns, which were characterized by senseless battles of attrition that generally failed to produce any decisive strategic effect on the war and only stiffened enemy resistance. True, a number of American commanders in the European theater of operations during the Second World War eventually adapted to progressive mechanized warfare, most notably during the race across France that followed the Normandy invasion and the subsequent conquest of Germany. The performances of both men and officers during these American campaigns were on a par with those of any other armored units on either side in the conflict; but such moments were brilliant and strategically vital exceptions to the depressing and devastating rule of a slow, linear advance that was punctuated by such brutally ineffective tactics as the firebombing of entire German cities, most notably Dresden in 1945—an episode that resulted in more than one hundred thousand fatalities.

Thus the ultimate lesson of the European war, to those outside observers for whom both freedom and the struggle to restore it were alien concepts (including, as we have seen, factions and countries in Asia, Africa, and

South America), was that Westerners were capable of waging wars that were not aimed at the devastation of civilian populations but that their violent and vengeful natures prevented them from doing so on anything other than a sporadic basis.

Such impressions were only reinforced by the Allied war against Japan. That empire's obscene rape not only of the city of Nanking but of much of China in the years prior to the American entrance into the war was something new, even in the Chinese experience. Though used to sustaining enormous and gruesome casualties during its own civil wars, the Chinese had not been subjected to such a systematic terrorizing of their population by outsiders since the invasion of the Mongol hordes. Certainly, the Japanese campaign, widely photographed and publicized throughout the world, was responsible for the accurate global perception of the Japanese army as a "horde" in its own right, with no ability or will to distinguish between enemy soldiers and civilians. And when this horde struck at the American Pacific fleet on December 7, 1941, the event threw the United States into a state of confusion and fear of a foreign threat such as it had not experienced since the burning of Washington in 1814.

Indeed, given that the attackers were of another ethnicity and that their customs were often radically different than those of the West (although they imitated the West in many ways, not least militarily), the clash of cultures involved in the American war with Japan seemed far more extreme than had that with the British or even with Nazi Germany. The depth of this difference was symbolized for many Americans by the Japanese choice of a sneak attack. While the United States had experienced assaults without warning at various points during both its expansion and its rise to world-power status, Pearl Harbor was seen as something particularly alien and threatening, more sinister even than the night attacks and murder raids of American Indian tribes during the frontier wars or than the sinking of the battleship *Maine* prior to the Spanish-American War. Indeed, for roughly eleven months after Pearl Harbor the severity of this sense of being victimized by a darkly mysterious and powerful enemy from the other side of the world threw America into roughly the same condition in which it found itself after September 11: confused, trying to marshal its forces without knowing exactly how, and not at all sure it could weather the storm intact.

The immediate sense of fear instilled by Pearl Harbor did slowly abate as both the Pacific and the European wars proceeded in America's favor; but that deeper sense of having been caught off guard by people who were in so many ways very different from Americans simply refused to dissipate. Attempts were made to eradicate it by striking back at the Japanese in much the same way that Japan had struck at America (or even worse), and those attempts began quickly: in April 1942, a small group of American bombers commanded by Lieutenant Colonel James Doolittle attacked Tokyo and several smaller Japanese communities, in an effort to both lift American morale and demonstrate to the Japanese that they, too, were vulnerable to attacks without warning, to terror from the sky. The unmentioned sticking point, however, was that the Japanese attack on Pearl Harbor, however much it had been a sneak attack launched by armed forces whose savagery was established, had also been an assault against a naval installation. There had been collateral damage and casualties, certainly, but they had been exactly that. The Doolittle raid, on the other hand— while ostensibly focused on military and industrial targets—involved the release of clusters of incendiary bombs over urban and suburban areas: inevitably civilians died, while very little damage of any real military value was done. In truth the raid's purpose from the moment of its inception was to undermine civilian support for the Japanese war effort, making the operation fit the definition of terrorism precisely. Like the later and vastly more extensive firebombing of German cities and numerous other long-range punitive actions undertaken during the war, the raids demonstrated that the United States and its allies were perfectly capable of acting in a manner that they claimed to be trying to eradicate. The age-old logic that to fight a dirty enemy one must become dirty oneself had surfaced again—and this time it had come to stay.

There was a moment at the conclusion of the Second World War when the United States could have chosen to disregard the dictates of so backward a philosophy. It came, of course, during the debate over whether or not to drop the atomic bomb and during the secondary argument over *where* to drop it. But for all the moral arguments raised and debated, the first issue was never really in doubt. As to the second, President Harry Truman did try to insist that the bomb be dropped—as the bombs of December 7, 1941, had been—on a military and not a civilian target, but for reasons that have never been entirely clear or agreed upon, it was ultimately unleashed on Hiroshima, a city with several hundred thousand civilian inhabitants but only ten thousand soldiers. (The city of Nagasaki, site of the second atomic drop, had only slightly greater military value.) While it could be argued that American bombers had already struck at all major Japanese military installations, leaving only minor ones such as those in Hiroshima and Nagasaki, it could also be argued that the choice of the two cities was evidence of the self-perpetuating vengeful nature of terror. (Such an argument gains credibility when one considers the extensive American firebombing of Japanese cities that characterized the final months of the war.)

In many ways the most pertinent fact about the use of atomic weapons against Japan was not that use per se, but the fact that comparatively few people subsequently questioned the justice or morality of it. There was a general sense of awe and dread throughout the world when the effects of the bombs were realized, to be sure; but the fact that those effects had been inflicted on Japan raised surprisingly few objections. Some have chalked this attitude up to racism, foolishly asserting that the Americans would never have dropped such bombs on Germany—when in fact, Franklin Roosevelt, before his death, had made it clear that he was prepared to do just that. The public outcry that would have been raised had Germany received the same punishment as Japan would likely have been similarly muted, and for the same reason: the two countries were not only terrorist states but expansionist terrorist states, and their grim fates (for firebombing was in many ways a horror equal to nuclear attack) were never considered by the vast majority of the world's citizens, and certainly not by those who had suffered most at their hands, as anything other than just.

All of which made it only more remarkable that the United States should have decided, when Germany and Japan finally lay prostrate, to rebuild both countries and make them viable nations once more. The generosity embodied in the Marshall Plan for Europe and the similar measures overseen in Japan by General Douglas MacArthur stand as the greatest acts of not only civilian but military generosity in the history of the world, as well as the greatest vindication of the argument that the tactics of terror must never be met with like behavior. For both Germany (or at least the part of the country controlled by the Western Allies) and Japan responded to this un-precedented decency by rejoining the community of constructive, civilized nations. America's decision to be magnanimous in victory undid a great deal of the cruel stupidity of the Allied civilian-bombing campaigns and brought both Japan and especially West Germany on board for the next great challenge that America and the West faced: that of Stalin's Russia, formerly a wartime ally but afterward an implacable philosophical and long-term foe.

The fight to contain the unarguably expansionist ter-ror of Stalinism would, sadly, have many deleterious and recidivist effects on the nations of the Western alliance, none worse than the reemergence and reinforcement of those self-defeating tendencies toward questionable be-havior that had been temporarily submerged by the Mar-shall Plan. In fact, during the coming battle with global communism, the West would sink to new depths of such questionable behavior in order to combat the tactics of their enemy. In so doing, they only further degraded their status in the eyes of many nations that were on the fringes of what constituted "world affairs."

This sad evolution was led, as were all post–Second World War Western developments and undertakings, by the United States. As soon as it became clear that Josef Stalin was indeed intent on undermining the interests of America and its allies (whenever he could do so without endangering his own or his nation's power, that is), the deep-seated anxiety that had been implanted in the American psyche by Pearl Harbor and had remained un-resolved following the successful conclusion of the war fi-nally found a new focus. The worldwide task before America and its Western allies was, it seemed to many, clear: having rid the world of two forms of expansionist totalitarianism, they must rid it of the next and of any others that might arise. The world must repeatedly be made safe for the development of freedom, a word that, in postwar public parlance, began to be used very loosely indeed. Its principal elements seemed to include not only (or even necessarily) democracy but capitalism and un-hindered international trade: the economic element in American political evangelism, always present but never before quite so blatant, was augmented and exposed con-siderably. Given this new elaboration of the fight to spread Western democratic capitalism, it might once again become necessary, some officials began to say, to adopt the tactics of the enemy, just as it had been "neces-sary" to adopt them against Nazi Germany and imperial Japan.

The logic was accepted among postwar Western leaders without anything that amounted to powerful, coherent opposition. In the United States, a new set of government agencies was quickly established, and old departments were reorganized to service the cause of what came to be called "national security." The concept was the obsession—indeed, the self-confessed "fetish"—of James Forrestal, a brilliant, rugged, and clinically deranged man of mystery who also happened to be secretary of the navy under Franklin Roosevelt and Harry Truman. Forrestal had a fear of communists in general and Russians in particular that was to eventually degenerate into paranoid schizophrenia; but before it did he pushed as hard as any man in Washington for the passage of the National Security Act of 1947. Under the terms of this act, the Defense Department was created (with Forrestal as its first secretary), and the Central Intelligence Agency and the National Security Council were authorized. These were and remain the three principal arms of what has come to be known as the "national-security state," a parallel government that exists beyond the power and prying eyes of voters and is devoted (supposedly) to security issues only—which was to say, after 1947, to the fight against Soviet-inspired communism and subversion.

The potential for abuse and danger inherent in the new arrangement was obvious from the outset: in advocating the creation of the three new departments, Forrestal had spoken of the need to fight Soviet "aggression" in terms that echoed both the National Convention of the French Revolution and Clausewitz: "We have to take into account our whole potential for war," he announced, "our mines, industry, manpower, research, and all the activities that go into normal civilian life. . . . This has to be a truly global effort." The general mood of the country, still powerfully influenced by Pearl Harbor, was in harmony with such thinking. True, statesmen of greater stature and less volatility than Forrestal occasionally voiced concerns. Dean Acheson, for example, Truman's incisive, forthright secretary of state, recorded that after reviewing the proposal for the Central Intelligence Agency he felt "the gravest forebodings" and warned the president that once it was established neither he "nor anyone else would be in a position to know what it was doing or to control it." But Forrestal and his camp adroitly exploited the nervousness of the nation, and the new national-security apparatus—the instruments through which America would match its enemies, shady move for shady move—was brought into being by Congress.

Many Americans doubtless felt reassured by the creation of such powerful new systems devoted to public safety; but James Forrestal was not, unfortunately, one of them. The billions of dollars that were freely and often unaccountably spent by his three new departments during their first two years did nothing to ease the secretary of defense's ever intensifying conviction that Stalin's schemes for undermining the West generally and America in particular were succeeding. It soon became clear to most people who knew and worked with Forrestal that his extreme fears were in fact a tale told, if not by an idiot, then at least by a very disturbed man, and that while they might signify more than nothing, they did not signify as much more as he had led people to believe they did. President Truman relieved Forrestal of his duties, after which the secretary underwent a severe mental collapse, insisting that a coalition of communists, Jews, and other members of the Truman administration were "after him." He was persuaded to enter Bethesda Naval Hospital, where, after brooding over the state of the world and his place in it, he one night threw himself out of an upper-story window.

The machinery Forrestal had overseen survived his death without a hitch, doing the work that he had planned for it: the Department of Defense kept the nation on a permanent wartime footing; the National Security Council provided the executive branch with a way to end-run the traditional (and constitutionally authorized) diplomatic jurisdiction of the State Department; and the Central Intelligence Agency planned and executed whatever covert operations it deemed necessary to thwart enemy plots and agents. (Occasionally it even paused to gather and analyze intelligence.) There were obvious reasons to think that any one of these branches, swept up in the excitement of keeping America safe, might overstep its bounds and actually *create* troubling foreign entanglements for the American government; but from the first it was the CIA that presented the gravest danger along these lines.

The Agency had inherited a strong operational bent from its wartime precursor, the Office of Strategic Services, in which many of its operatives had served. A continuity of style soon became apparent: in 1953, the CIA oversaw the toppling of an Iranian premier who it believed was too close to the Soviets, and subsequently reinstated that country's controversial shah. In the following year, Guatemala received similar treatment, its leftist-leaning head of state falling to a near-comical plot engineered by the CIA. The American president at the time, Dwight Eisenhower, had no objections to such schemes, provided the CIA kept him abreast of impending events of truly critical importance; but there had already been cause to think that the Agency was not taking this research and analysis role as seriously as it was its operational adventures. The CIA had been unable to provide warning of the Soviet blockade of West Berlin in 1948, for example, or of the North Korean invasion of South Korea in 1950; and it had subsequently downplayed the possibility that communist China would enter the latter conflict. These errors had resulted in enormous American casualties; yet when reminded later of such things, CIA defenders could be counted on to point to such triumphs as Iran and Guatemala, the only real effects of which had been the alienation of large segments of those nations' respective populations. And there were darker rumors, too, which grew in number as the years went by: the CIA was training anticommunist guerrillas in various parts of the world; tampering with the economies of countries that were not strident enough in their opposition to Moscow; and even training assassins to remove leftist or simply independent leaders of foreign nations.

The CIA, in short, was beginning to bear an uncomfortable resemblance to an organ of state terror.

By 1956, Eisenhower—though he had been aware of many of the CIA's activities and had approved at least some of them—had grown concerned enough over the general trend of its behavior and the criticism that such behavior inspired to order a report on the agency's covert operations. The job of assembling the study was given, in a moment of supreme historical aptness, to none other than James Doolittle, the air-force lieutenant colonel who in 1942 had introduced the Japanese to the American version of Roman punitive raiding. The phrasing of the document that Doolittle eventually submitted could not have been more consistent with his earlier job of terroriz-

ing Japanese civilians in retaliation for the crimes of an
emperor and an army over which they had absolutely no
control.

"It is now clear," wrote Doolittle, who had risen to become a lieutenant general, "that we are facing an implacable enemy whose avowed object is world domination by
whatever means and at whatever cost. There are no rules
in such a game. Hitherto acceptable norms of human behavior do not apply. If the United States is to survive,
long-standing American concepts of 'fair play' must be re-
considered. . . . It may be necessary that the American
people be made acquainted with, understand and support
this fundamentally repugnant philosophy."

The report amounted to official recognition that what
had originally been sold to the American public as an organization that would increase their leaders' knowledge
of the nature and plans of prospective and established
enemies had in fact become (as Dean Acheson had predicted it would) a highly operational force beyond the
control of any government official, including the president. Furthermore, in tone the report reflected a disturbing
attitude—indeed, an inexplicably dominating fear—
among American leaders that somehow, given a free
choice, most people in the world would choose Soviet
values over American, unless they were actively convinced
or coerced to do otherwise.

For the next half century, the CIA would continue fo-

cusing enormous amounts of attention and funds on
covert operations, while missing calls on larger, truly vital
world developments. The growing rift between communist China and the Soviet Union during the 1950s and
1960s; the decay of the British empire and the rise of important indigenous political movements in its former
colonies; and the economic rise of Japan and Western Europe were all fundamental global changes that the CIA
proved incapable of predicting or adequately appreciat-
ing. Instead, it continued to focus on narrow operational
schemes, many of them simply embarrassing, some of
them—such as the Bay of Pigs fiasco in Cuba in 1961—
genuinely threatening to American prestige and interests.
And through it all, there continued to be those darker rumors: of poisoned hypodermic needles sent to eliminate
an unwanted leader of the Congo; of joint operations
with the Mafia to eliminate Fidel Castro; of assassins
who, when they committed their crimes, conveniently
destroyed all traces of their connection to the Agency;
and of more paramilitary training of anticommunist
groups, with no regard given to what political system or
philosophy such groups might actually be advocating.

Increasingly criticized for its failures as the years
passed, the CIA formulated what amounted to a trump-
card excuse: when one of its operations failed, its officers
invariably explained, the public found out about it, but
the Agency's successes were always kept secret. The fact

that various directors of the CIA had never actually experienced any trouble openly discussing many of those successes never gave the lie to this rote rationalization. The CIA's charmed life and cursed operations went on, all the while deepening the global impression of the United States that had been fostered during the Second World War: America was a country that knew how to make limited and progressive war, but it all too often chose a different path.

Certainly, the conventional forces of the United States did little to counter this perception. The American military's path to its strategic, tactical, and moral nadir, the Vietnam War, is not at all difficult to trace from this perspective. The taste for strategic bombing that had been sharpened over Germany and Japan led to the creation of an enormous—and enormously expensive—fleet of B-52 bombers, the commanders of which were anxious to prove that America's enemies could be beaten into submission from an untouchable distance without American servicemen ever experiencing any casualties. American ground units, too, continued to bask in their European triumphs, building bigger and better tanks, which promised to be of absolutely no use in the rugged countries that were usually the battlegrounds between American and Soviet influence, while refusing to adequately develop large-scale unconventional units with which to fight and otherwise operate in such locales. Indeed, unconventional warfare in general was left to those special-forces units that had always played an elite and therefore unusual role in the modern American military. The idea that warfare had changed in a world populated by two superpowers and dozens of lesser powers—that it had in fact come to resemble the colonial wars of the nineteenth century more than the world wars of the twentieth—failed to take a dominating hold among the officer corps of the American military; and indeed, it never would.

Thus, America marched incrementally but purpose-fully into southeast Asia, eager but unprepared, believing that it had an important job to do but unaware that that job was largely a figment of its own continuing anxieties. In fighting a war for which they had never been ade-quately trained, American servicemen were to acquit themselves with remarkable bravery and character, given the utter strategic, conceptual, and organizational confu-sion that plagued their superiors, as well as the chaos that surrounded them at every turn—to say nothing of the dedication and genius of the enemy they were facing. The leaders of the North Vietnamese cause, Ho Chi Minh and his military commander, Vo Nguyen Giap, were two of the most accomplished masters of guerrilla and psycho-logical warfare that the world has ever seen; they were also, within their own region, masters of the tactics of ter-ror. Yet Ho's and Giap's perspicacity was further demon-strated by the fact that they never dispatched agents of terror into America itself, a tactic that would (as we have, sadly, learned recently) have been easy enough to execute but that would likely have brought the full weight of the American military machine down on their heads. Ho knew that his country was winning the war: North Vietnam and the Vietcong were slowly wearing down America's patience and will, and much as some Americans were growing increasingly discouraged by the casualties the nation was sustaining, others were growing ashamed of and alarmed by the increasingly terrorist tactics of their own military and intelligence forces.

For whatever else one can say about the American effort in Vietnam—about the extraordinary bravery of many American troops and about the genuinely decent intentions with which many men and women offered to serve—the orders issued by many senior American officials and the behavior of operational American intelligence organizations (most notably, once again, the CIA) *did* constitute warfare waged against civilians for political purposes. The carpet bombing of North Vietnam and pervasive use of napalm throughout the region; the secret bombings of and incursions into Cambodia, pet schemes of Henry Kissinger and Richard Nixon; the CIA's notorious Phoenix assassination program, whose true scope, purpose, and victims may never be known but which was infamous throughout both South and North Vietnam; all of these and more were tactics designed to break the will of the Vietnamese to fight. Being essentially terrorist in nature, however, they had the precisely opposite effect. (A very few American statesmen, most prominently and ubiquitously Henry Kissinger, have affected awareness of this inevitable outcome. Kissinger claims to have urged that the strategic bombing of Cambodia with B-52s *not* be directed against civilian targets, a claim that is remarkable either for its disingenuousness or for the fact that a Harvard-trained historian could be unaware that it is *impossible* for strategic-bombing campaigns to avoid civilian casualties.)

The principal reason that the United States was defeated in Vietnam was not the inadequacy of its military effort or the failure of its soldiers or even the superiority of the enemy it faced. For the effort was enormous, American soldiers fought well, and the North Vietnamese, while dogged and well led, themselves admitted that they could not have won without the deterioration of domestic morale that occurred within the United States. And that deterioration was not due to media influence or to social degeneracy: it was due to the fact that such American leaders as John Kennedy, Lyndon Johnson, Richard Nixon, and Henry Kissinger had followed James Doolittle's advice and given themselves over to a repugnant and self-defeating philosophy. They had become terrorists, and all in the cause of a political fallacy—for when North Vietnam finally triumphed, there were no waves of communist troops suddenly landing on the shores of Hawaii, as Lyndon Johnson had once publicly predicted. There was simply a reunited Vietnam (one that, in time, developed an enormous appetite for American consumer goods), a great many dead soldiers and civilians, and a heightened international perception of America as a nation that had no difficulty matching terror with terror.

That perception bred powerful resentment in many parts of the world, places where the continued American (and more generally Western) rationalization that their objectionable tactics were being employed in the name of freedom was rejected. In such places, a new response to the overwhelming military might of the West began to emerge, especially after the Vietnam War: a particularly vicious type of unlimited warfare that would soon become known as international political terrorism.

CHAPTER TEN

SHAKE HANDS WITH MURDER

Thus the twentieth century has been dominated by the unlimited, popular form of international conflict that first achieved a dispiritingly complete form during the wars of the French Revolution. At no point between the death of Queen Victoria in 1901 and the dawn of the next millennium was there any meaningful international attempt to enforce the various codes for military conduct that were worked out first during the several Geneva conferences and later by the United Nations. Nearly every country in the world has followed Great Britain's 1914 precedent by unilaterally rewriting or rejecting any provision of any agreement that has stood in the way of its private pursuit of supposed or actual "national security." Such has been the example of the greater to the lesser powers and vice versa: high-minded agreements are laudable, but war is war, and, in William Tecumseh Sherman's words, "you cannot refine it."

The fact that this statement is wrong—that Sherman's words were, as he himself privately acknowledged, more a self-serving rationalization than the revelation of any true, natural state of belligerency—has escaped nearly every twentieth-century leader. Worse, the fatally misleading philosophies that have developed out of total war have prompted many nations and groups to adopt policies and practices that have proved intensely self-destructive. Military history teaches us that in reality war *can* be "refined," provided that such refinement tends toward the more complete realization of a given combatant's political aims. Not Oliver Cromwell or Frederick the Great or any other early modern leader who advanced the conduct of war from the merely bestial to the progressive devised his principles solely out of the kind of moral concern that preoccupied St. Augustine and Grotius. Rather, reformation offered those pragmatic secular leaders a way to achieve their goals more quickly, more completely, and less expensively. Similarly self-serving yet limited and progressive tactics could have offered the same results to later generations of soldiers: there is no reason why the commanders of America's Civil War, for instance, could not have learned from such historical examples as Cromwell and Frederick, as Prussia's Helmuth von Moltke did—except that the Americans were hostage to a national tradition of unlimited warfare, which bred a complementary lack of military imagination. It was this tradition that gave Sherman's words the ring of revealed truth and that set the global example for the twentieth century.

As the process of following that example unfolded, a second and perhaps even more pernicious fallacy about the nature of total war crept into world affairs. The French Revolution had established the precedent of an unlimited conflict that was also a popular war. Popular wars tend by nature to be unlimited, for a people fighting in the name of a cause that has a personal dimension for each of them is not likely to have undergone the sort of strict discipline that produces soldiers capable of fighting limited wars. (Even if, as in the cases of the opposing armies of the Second World War, such disciplined soldiers *can* be produced, the emotion of their cause is likely to inform their battlefield behavior as much as their training, as it did for both Allied and Axis troops, who were guilty of frequent breaches of military conduct, particularly the wanton execution of prisoners.) But if all popular wars are unlimited, does it conversely stand that all unlimited wars are popular? The logic is so tempting that it has led many nations and peoples down a path to tragedy and disaster. For along with being tempting, it is also utterly and tragically false.

The most significant twentieth-century example of

this falsehood, a precedent that has been echoed countless times in nations on every continent, is the case of Ireland. The centuries following Cromwell's misguided and cruel exploits on that island saw the wider expansion and stronger establishment of British Protestant authority over the largely Catholic indigenous population. Laws that governed Ireland became increasingly discriminatory, and although there were occasional uprisings—including one inspired, in the late eighteenth century, by the French Revolution—most if not all were put down with a ruthlessness that was in keeping with Cromwell's. The Great Famine of the 1840s was also handled by London in ways that could easily have been interpreted as genocidal but that were more often simply callous; that callousness, however, was sufficient to ignite the various and violent disruptive actions of the Fenian Brotherhood, a group of not only Irish natives but Irish Americans, whose enthusiasm never failed to exceed their skill and effectiveness.

During the balance of the nineteenth century and the opening of the twentieth, Irish discontent was more constructively channeled through the Irish Nationalist Party, which held, by the outbreak of the First World War, some eighty seats in Parliament. The INP fought first and foremost for home rule (Irish administration of Ireland within the British commonwealth as a prelude to independence), as well as for the particular rights of different classes of Irishmen, especially those tenant farmers who worked for British and Protestant landlords under grossly unfair terms and shamefully unhealthy conditions. By 1914, it looked as if the INP would indeed win "free state" status for Catholic southern Ireland; but then the Great War broke out and negotiations were put on hold, the INP voting to participate in the fight against the Central Powers.

By 1916, approximately sixty thousand Irish soldiers were serving in France. But the radical groups outside the INP that had long been campaigning, violently and otherwise, for Irish independence were not willing to give priority to the fight in Europe. In the early hours of Easter Monday, members of three groups—the Irish Republican Brotherhood, along with its ancillary organizations, Sinn Fein and the Irish Volunteers—set up armed positions at key points in central Dublin, focusing on the general post office. There they proclaimed an end to London's rule and the establishment of an independent Irish republic, at the same time calling for a general uprising. The call went unheeded. The vast majority of Dubliners and Irishmen were not willing to battle police and occupational troops, and some even resented the radicals' presumption in speaking for them. *The Freeman's Journal,* a nationalist newspaper, decried what it called "an armed assault against the will and decision of the Irish nation, itself constitutionally ascertained through its proper representatives." The rebellion was put down, and the leaders tried. And then the British made a terrible mistake.

Instead of recognizing that the rebellion had enjoyed only limited support among the Irish and that its leaders would therefore best be dealt with by keeping them quietly locked up, London permitted more severe penalties to be pronounced. The Dublin military commanders were allowed to court-martial and shoot the ringleaders, an act that was an affront to even moderate Irish citizens. George Bernard Shaw stated that Britain was "canonizing the prisoners," and he was not exaggerating. The Irish now had a set of nationalist martyrs, but, even more ominously, terror had escalated in Ireland, evolving into one of its most counterproductive forms: disproportionate and vengeful military justice.

Moderates among the Irish revolutionaries were now eclipsed, and the movement for independence fell to the leadership of Sinn Fein and its chiefs: Eamon De Valera, Arthur Griffith, and Michael Collins. In another example of its apparent inability to read the Irish situation correctly, the London government proceeded to arrest De Valera, Griffith, and others but failed to lay hands on Michael Collins—and it was Collins who best understood how to organize an unconventional campaign of resistance. He shuffled the Irish Volunteers into a new form, called the Irish Republican Army, rounded up all the arms he could find, and trained his men and women in the tactics of ambush and assassination. Their achievements were savage and impressive: hundreds of British soldiers were killed, British officials and their Irish informers lived in perpetual fear of execution, and by 1920 Ireland was in a state that seemed to border on open rebellion, even war.

Michael Collins has been intensely romanticized by novelists, Hollywood, and the public, but it must be remembered that the tactics he devised eventually proliferated to such an extent that killing British troops and their leaders was given priority over sparing civilian lives. And in this, he set the pattern not only for his own undoing but for Irish violence to this day. There was nothing inherently regressive or barbaric about killing British soldiers or assassinating political and military leaders—Sinn Fein and the IRA had, after all, announced themselves to be at war with British authority, and such guerrilla tactics in wartime were completely legitimate. (The fact that the British refused to acknowledge this state of war was not only immaterial but foolish. Not unlike the American response to the Al Qaeda organization over the last decade, it substituted moral outrage for effective response.) Nor could anyone expect that, during such a state of war, there would not be some civilian casualties. But Collins's irregulars soon began to *cultivate* civilian deaths—along with the physical and psychological intimidation of noncombatants—as a way to spread disorder and fear and thus disrupt the ability of the British authorities to govern effectively. In other words, they randomly targeted non-combatants for political purposes, thus embracing—indeed, systematizing and formally elaborating—principles of terrorism.

Tragic results abounded: innocent people began dying at a rate that grew close to that of British forces, but worse yet, the rebels' efforts along these lines, like the British execution of the Easter Rebellion leaders, became utterly gratuitous and self-defeating. Collins's guerrilla tactics were sound enough on their own—and the British, with their extreme reactions, were making themselves sufficiently unpopular—for Sinn Fein and the IRA to realistically think that in a matter of years they could bring about profound change. But the spread of terror meant that the British suspended negotiations (reopened after the end of the First World War) and sent in tough new occupational troops of a wholly different and nastier breed than their regular soldiers. The British prime minister, David Lloyd George, unofficially said that he would not "shake hands with murder." In addition, popular resentment of the radical nationalists not only remained but began to grow, thus giving the lie to the IRA's claim to being the single most legitimate voice of the Irish people. The practical result of Collins's terror campaign was an offer by the British in 1921 of free-state status: nothing more than what the nationalists could have had in

1914. His popularity among the people sagging, Collins was forced to accept, and for doing so, he was murdered by the same breed of extremists that he had created.

It is here that the Irish example offers the clearest exposure of the confusion between unlimited and popular war. By crossing the line from guerrilla action into terrorism, Sinn Fein and the IRA had definitely placed their conflict in the category of unlimited war, two of the principal characteristics of which are a refusal to recognize any distinction between soldiers and civilians and a willingness to deliberately target the latter. As we have seen, popular wars were almost by definition unlimited; but again, was the reverse logic applicable? Was a war popular simply by virtue (if such it can be called) of being unlimited, of involving every element of society? The answer, of course, was no: such reasoning was sheer, deadly sophistry, and it remains so to this day. Certainly, the terrorism of Sinn Fein and what has, over the intervening decades, come to be called the Provisional and later "Real" IRA may be popular with drunken Americans who thoughtlessly finance the purchase of weapons and their illicit transport into Ireland, just as it may be popular among barroom Irish "patriots" who, when sober, have no wish to be anywhere near a battlefield. But among the average citizens that live and work in such an atmosphere, "the causes"—first of Irish statehood, then of Irish union with those provinces of Northern Ireland over which

Britain retained authority after recognizing, during their *general* retreat from empire, southern Ireland's declaration of full independence in 1949—gained and continue to gain no ground through terror.

This fact is thoroughly demonstrated by the current state of Irish peace negotiations, which find the IRA no closer to its goal of unification after thirty years of renewed and abominable terror, both on their part and on the part of their Protestant Irish enemies. Thus the declaration that Gerry Adams, current head of Sinn Fein, "bombed his way to the peace table"—a slogan popular not only with barroom authorities but among supposedly responsible scholars of history and terrorism—is revealed as further lethal sophistry: the British have always been willing to talk to the IRA, but they are not today any more willing to make concessions to terrorism than they have ever been. In truth, the IRA's greatest hope for the advancement of their cause lies in the extent to which their Unionist enemies are willing to imitate their tactics and thus alienate the public. But as for the terrorists over whom such leaders as Adams either cannot or will not exercise control, they have gained nothing more through such tactics than did Michael Collins. Collins's one chance for greatness, for true achievement, lay in limiting the Irish cause's violence to a guerrilla campaign aimed at British soldiers and officials; and indeed, during the fleeting moments when he was able to so limit it, he came within reach of remarkable results. But when he let the conflict bleed over into terrorism, all the ground he had gained was lost, and he proved far less effective an advocate for Irish rights than the members of the INP, who had struggled for so long in Parliament.

The most powerful effect of Sinn Fein and the IRA during the first half of the twentieth century lay not in their actual accomplishments but in their propaganda and legend: they took great pains to travel the world portraying themselves as having been responsible for any and all advances of the Irish cause. Many nationalist or simply disaffected groups in other countries believed them—for, again, the logic that an unlimited war must be a popular war, that terrorism could work and had worked, was seductive, since civilians were far easier and less dangerous targets than soldiers. In subsequent years, it became a hallmark of guerrilla groups all over the world, when they expanded their operations into the realm of terror, to represent their causes as being popular by virtue of their violence being unlimited. Indeed, another, reverse ratio soon became established, one that had enormous destructive potential: the less popular a given cause actually was, the more necessary it became to use the tactics of unlimited war on as broad a scale as possible, in order to create the illusion of popularity.

It is for this reason that we find the word *popular* used repeatedly—indeed, to an almost comic extent—in the

hyperbolic titles of dozens of revolutionary or simply terrorist organizations. Like the Soviet state that trained so
many of them, these groups believed that such repetition
would foster acceptance of their claim to legitimacy
among the nations and citizens of the world; and no one
subscribed to such troublesome and flawed thinking
more than the various organizations that struggled, beginning in the 1930s, to gain control of the Middle Eastern region called Palestine.

Both Britain and France had made specific promises
of independent statehood to the Muslim tribes of Arabia,
Palestine, and Syria during the First World War, in order
to gain their assistance in fighting the Ottoman empire.
Those various ancient tribes had long since wearied of
Ottoman rule, viewing the Turks as corrupt, lapsed Muslims who allowed themselves such proscribed indulgences
as alcohol. (It should be remembered that it was in Arabia, particularly among the extremist Wahhabi sect, that
Muslim fundamentalism had always flourished.) Puritani-
cal religious observation and clan loyalties had steadily
superseded loyalty to Constantinople, among the Arabs,
and prompted many of them to take up arms and help
the British eject the Turks from their region.

Even before the war was over, however, the Arabs
learned that the Europeans had been lying: an agreement
between France and Britain on how to divide the area between them (Syria and southeast Turkey would go to

France, Jordan and Iraq to Britain) for the purpose of creating "mandates"—a vague term for zones of influence in
which each respective power would hold some administrative and a great deal of economic control—had been
reached in 1916. The Arabs scarcely had time to recover
from this discovery before another came: the British intended to support the idea of creating a Zionist homeland
in Palestine, which, under the terms of the Anglo-French
agreement, was supposed to be an international zone.
Both of these agreements were phrased so loosely that the
British and French representatives assigned to the infuriated Arab tribes were able to double-talk and cajole their
way through the conclusion of peace and on into the
1920s. In the midst of this diplomatic chicanery, Palestine never achieved the status of international territory:
the British retained control, as they did in Jordan to
the east. But by 1928, Jordan had been granted self-
government, while Iraq had actually been made an independent state (although the British secured for themselves
favored trade status). Yet Palestine remained stuck in the
mandate system, largely because, its inhabitants correctly
believed, that system gave Britain the power to manipu-
late questions of land ownership in favor of the European
Zionists that they, under heavy pressure from British and
other European Jewish lobbies, were helping relocate to
the area.

By 1933, with Hitler in power in Germany, somewhere between fifteen and thirty thousand Jews a year were emigrating to Palestine under British protection. In 1936, the Palestinians went on general strike, demanding a full stop to Jewish immigration, as well as self-government. The British answered with a royal commission, which eventually rejected the appeal for self-government and recommended that Palestine be partitioned into two parts, one Arab, one Jewish. Sixty percent of the arable land in Palestine was to go to the Jewish sector, which held 30 percent of Palestine's population. Deadly violence broke out; and in response, the British put together another royal commission report, this one recommending that the British keep more land under their own authority and give less to both Jews and Arabs.

At the close of the 1930s, the Jewish communities in Palestine—alarmed at increasing Arab calls for an end to Jewish immigration, along with accompanying Palestinian threats against any Arab citizen or national leader who did not support their cause—made the fateful decision to expand the membership of two armed bands that were already defending Jewish settlers: the Irgun, and its aptly titled offshoot, the Stern Gang. Arab anger had bred violence and murder in Palestine; but it was the Jews who brought organized, paramilitary terror into the region. The goal of the Irgun and the Stern Gang was an all-Jewish state of Israel that would extend from the mountains of Lebanon to the Suez Canal and east to include

Jordan. Their ideas on how this could—indeed, must—be achieved were advertised in their logo: a raised fist holding a rifle, below which were the words "Only Thus." Their groups were a synthesis of and improvement on the cell-based organization of various revolutionary groups devised by the Bolsheviks for their takeover of Russia and the subsequent spread of communist subversion throughout the world. Irgun operations were planned by individual units that often knew nothing of one another's activities; and those activities were not limited to protecting settlers who were already established residents. The Irgun and the Stern Gang provided protection for the illegal entrance of tens of thousands of new Jewish residents in 1938–1939 alone, and their tactics included everything from beatings to bombings to murder. That they were accomplished at their work was reflected in the remarkably lopsided death toll during the long months of heavy violence. By one independent count, the British lost 77 people and the Jews 250; the Arabs, however, sustained some 3,500 fatalities.

The ease with which the Jewish terrorists turned to murder and mayhem was perhaps understandable, given what was happening in Europe and the tales that were being brought to Palestine by immigrants. The Irgun and the Stern Gang sought to augment through violence the world's meager sympathy for the plight of both European and Palestinian Jews by creating the image not of armed

212   CALEB CARR

land-grabbers (which many of them were) but of a people
forcefully defending their homeland. In other words, like
the IRA and Sinn Fein, the Jewish terrorists believed that
they could propagate the idea of a popular war by engaging in unlimited tactics; and like their Irish counterparts,
they were wrong.

The British could see that both the plight of the Arabs
and the general level of violence in Palestine were reaching unacceptable extremes. Further, they had no wish to
alienate the rulers of the oil-rich countries to the east and
south. (Not that they needed to have any anxiety on that
score: most leaders of Muslim states, then as now, had little more than symbolic interest in the fate of the Palestinian Arabs.) In 1939, the London government therefore
delivered an extraordinary volte-face called the White
Paper, in which it admitted that its previous policies had
been unfair to the Arabs, that Jewish immigration and
settlement needed to slow down, and that the British
themselves should, over the following decade, get out,
leaving the Arabs and the Jews to run Palestine jointly "in
such a way as to ensure that the essential interests of each
community are safeguarded."

It was an unprecedented moment, in a variety of important ways: the still proud British empire was admit-
ting its wrongs, abdicating its position, and trying to
make amends to an indigenous population that had been
treated unfairly while still holding the door open to a sec-

ond people that was being unthinkably victimized in Europe. And, like all sensible compromises in the long history of Palestinian-Jewish relations, it got absolutely nowhere. The Arabs rejected the British plan sullenly, while the Jews stepped up their paramilitary organization and training and continued their assassinations of important British officials, Arab leaders, and even moderate Jews, all as the Second World War raged. Following the war, the campaign of Jewish terror reached its peak on July 22, 1946, when the Irgun—commanded by future Israeli prime minister Menahem Begin—blew up an entire wing of the famously beautiful King David Hotel in Jerusalem. Ninety people died: and once again, the victims were Arabs, Britons, and Jews alike. Given such behavior, and given that they had long planned to leave anyway, the British informed the new United Nations that they intended to relinquish administration of Palestine to international control in 1947; and the UN—unable, as was much of the world, to separate what had happened to the Jews in Europe from what the Jews had long been doing in Palestine—subsequently came up with a new partition plan that gave even more prime territory to Jewish settlers.

During the months following the British departure, the Jews fought a war for the establishment of the State of Israel that saw many heroic deeds achieved by an enormous cross-section of their people. The Irgun and the

Stern Gang, however, continued the murderous ways that had turned the British—once the Jews' most powerful protectors in the region—against them. Menahem Begin still believed that murdering civilians and hurling bombs into crowds of Arab shoppers would somehow break the Arabs' spirits and provoke sympathy for the Jews among the world community. He continued to be mistaken, and the global reaction grew particularly bad when Begin ordered his followers to focus their attention once again on targets in Jerusalem, hoping to create enough terror in that triply holy city to force the United Nations to drop its plans to place it under international supervision. So negative was the press created by the Irgun that even David Ben-Gurion, head of the Israeli cause, privately condemned their killing of civilians. But Begin ignored the censure, and later, after an armistice was declared, he denounced the agreement and kept fighting, this time instigating an armed showdown among Jews and posing a threat to the new Israeli government. The government won, but the strain of vicious terrorism that the Irgun had bred into the Israeli character would never be removed. Worst of all, it would inspire vengeful imitation among the Palestinian Arabs.

When the Palestinians formed those groups whose names were in time to become so familiar—the Popular Front for the Liberation of Palestine, al-Fatah (or the Palestinian Liberation Movement), and its close but less openly military associate, the Palestine Liberation Organization—they took as one of their organizational and operational models the Irgun. The Palestinians also received training in the Soviet Union, from which the Irgun had borrowed so many techniques. Had they not witnessed over many years the murderous efficiency of the Irgun, the Palestinians might have been tempted to choose a different path; but anger, desperation, and impatience took them down the same road, and inevitably, the results of their decision were also similar.

In a climate of commonplace terror, the Palestinians needed to put some sort of distinctive spin on their own activities. They found it when they made the leap from victimizing only Israelis to attacking citizens of any nations that they felt were aiding Israel, which eventually included a considerable list of powerful countries. But as time went on, the head of al-Fatah (and later of the Palestine Liberation Organization), Yasir Arafat, focused his group's violent attention on one nation in particular: the United States, the first country to have granted de facto recognition to Israel when it declared its independence and thereafter its chief supplier of money and arms. Arafat's focus astounded and confused many Americans, but, having endured what they saw—correctly, in many cases—as Israeli terror, the Palestinians were simply declaring the Americans guilty by association, supply, and financing. Surprising as this idea may have been at the time, it should not be now: it is very similar to the approach the United States has promulgated with respect to those nations that harbor, finance, or otherwise support current terrorist organizations. In addition, it was Arafat's belief (along with certain members of the Popular Front for the Liberation of Palestine) that his movement would be more widely seen as a popular and therefore legitimate one if it spread the tactics of unlimited war outside the Middle East and had the ensuing actions covered by television; and the United States *was* the world capital of mass media. In this way, Arafat hoped, the PLO and especially he himself would come to be seen as the representatives and leaders of a movement as valid as any popular struggle for independence in history. Arafat was taking the Irish formula worldwide, all the while forgetting that the IRA—though its violence did gain newspaper and later television attention—had made no real headway in its political struggle.

Similarly and predictably, neither Arafat nor any other Palestinian leader was ever able to make significant progress in the court of public opinion by victimizing Americans or other non-Israeli civilians or by killing Israeli noncombatants. Indeed, the only periods during which Palestinian organizations were able to drum up meaningful Western support came when they engaged Israeli conventional military forces—or, as in the case of Black September in 1970, other Arab military units. The internecine war between Arafat's *fedayeen*—"those who are ready to sacrifice themselves"—and King Hussein of Jordan's Western-modeled Arab Legion happened to co-incide with an unusual multiple-airplane hijacking by the PFLP, during which the Palestinians removed the passengers and released many of them before destroying only the planes and then opening communication with reporters and making demands for the release of various comrades in Europe. They thus sent a signal that their priority, even their intention, might not be murder but rather serious international attention for their plight. The tactic served them, as it resulted in not only the release of their comrades but considerable television interview time, which would likely not have been possible had they gone on a killing spree aboard the planes. Combined with television images of *fedayeen* being slaughtered by Hussein's troops—who, it was hinted, might be supported by Israeli air strikes—Black September had the strange but ultimately positive effect of diminishing Arafat's stature within the community of Arab governments but enhancing it in other, potentially more important parts of the world, as well as among the younger generation of Palestinians.

More recently, the men orchestrating and the youths participating in the Palestinian *intifada* movement have also discovered that the world is willing to pay attention to—and even admire—their actions when they take the form of guerrilla attacks against the Israeli military. Public-opinion polls in America alone showed a significant spike in favor of the Palestinians when the *intifada* campaigns were launched and the airwaves became dominated by pictures of young men armed with nothing more than rocks and slings facing up to combat troops and riot police. The biblical parallel was obvious and effective; but change in American and Israeli policy did not follow the change in American public opinion fast enough to suit the Palestinians, who have since resorted to the tactic of blowing up Israeli civilians—specifically, on some occasions, young people—with equally young suicide bombers. It is a doubly bestial and doubly counterproductive tactic, one that has led to a predictable plummet in the perception of Palestinians among Westerners; and an equally predictable maintenance of pro-Israel policies.

Thus it can be safely said that the experiences and tactics of radical Irish nationalists and Jewish and Palestinian guerrillas and terrorists have mirrored one another throughout the century—and led to frustration and failure for all parties, due to their inability to stay the course of limiting their tactics. At least one leader of the movement for a unified Ireland, Sinn Fein's Gerry Adams, at last seems ready to comprehend this fact and to commit to the disarmament of his people as a condition for meaningful peace talks. Yasir Arafat, on the other hand, has displayed far less prudence by reaching once again for violence. The Israelis, in turn, have answered with increased repression and land-grabbing, and it now seems unlikely that Arafat will ever be able to achieve the concessions that were available to him before his youngest soldiers began strapping explosives to their bodies and becoming "martyrs" in Israeli nightclubs and cafés. Like a Middle Eastern Michael Collins, Arafat seems destined to see his long campaign of terror go for naught, and his abandonment of more limited guerrilla warfare revealed as a tragic mistake. He, too, will then, quite possibly, suffer assassination at the hands—again, like Collins—of the more extreme elements of his own cause. But Collins, at least, gave his life for home rule; if Arafat cannot control his suicidal murderers, he may lose even that to an increasingly vengeful, angry Israeli society that has demonstrated a pronounced capacity for making war against civilians. (Indeed, how else could both Menahem Begin and the alleged war criminal Ariel Sharon have attained the office of prime minister?)

The central cautionary lessons embodied by Michael Collins and Yasir Arafat—that reaching for unlimited tactics does not gain a movement the validity of a genuinely popular cause; that the impatient, vain, and destructive instinct that makes otherwise exceptional men attempt such tactics brings about only their own downfalls; and finally that there can be no substitute, in any independence movement, for the courage and ability to either engage enemy troops immediately or wait (as such truly great guerrilla leaders as Mao Zedong and Ho Chi Minh did) until the opportunity is right for such engagement—have been taught over and over around the world during the twentieth century. In the process, countless would-be revolutionaries have been revealed as mere terrorists. The pattern has been remarkably consistent, down to, again, the seemingly superficial but actually quite purposeful use of the word *popular* in the names of nearly all such failed movements. Indeed, an interesting transformation has occurred concerning the use of that particular word: *popular* is often no longer an indication of a noble struggle against oppression but a dead giveaway of a usually fraudulent, often dangerous, sometimes mentally deranged (as in the case of the various small European terror cliques), and almost always doomed group that stands for little save a desperate craving for power and recognition.

Ultimately, then, in examining these additional methods of warfare against civilians in the twentieth century, we come upon still more lessons that closely resemble many of those that characterized such warfare in the Roman era, and indeed in every intervening generation and century. It would not be fair to say that humanity has never learned from these lessons; but the knowledge gleaned has proved fleeting, while a return to the belief in the power of unlimited destruction has come to seem inevitable. The behavior of the United States over the last twenty years offers examples of both this transitory learning and the more habitual reliance on destructive or total war; and these examples have enormous implications for how we should face the challenge that is now before us.

PROFIT OR PRESERVATION?

Over the last twenty years, the United States has become particularly identified, with much justification, as the most powerful force behind the propagation throughout the world of Western values, the Western economic system, and Western popular culture. During this same period, America has risen to become not only the leading but the only true military superpower; and the connection between these two developments has not been lost on the people who live outside the primary ring of industrial and technological development, in countries where those same Western values have increasingly held sway, both by invitation and via the less-than-subtle imperatives of international capitalism. The steady erosion of indigenous traditions that is the inevitable result of this cultural and economic penetration has increasingly been seen as a process that enjoys the protection of the mighty American military machine. As a result, those who would protect traditional values—or who simply wish to advance political agendas that cannot be made to fit under the rubric of "multinationalism"—have reached for the only weapons that they feel can cause American society, long inured to airplane hijackings and car bombs, to sit up and take notice: weapons of mass destruction. These weapons can be machinery and devices not originally designed for belligerent purposes, as in the case of airliners used as offensive missiles, or they can be carefully and patiently designed and cultured, as in the case of biological weapons. Either way, international terrorism has taken a sudden, significant leap in its strategy and particularly its tactics in order to match the dominant American military role in the world.

There can be little question that both that strategy and those tactics will prove self-defeating: the current agents of terror have unwisely chosen to ignore the lessons of similar campaigns (although it is perhaps unrealistic to think that people who spend their time immersed in medieval religious rumination and bomb schematics would do anything else). Instead, they have elected to deliberately victimize civilians in a manner and on a scale not seen in generations, perhaps centuries. In so doing, the organizers, sponsors, and foot soldiers of every terrorist group involved in the September 11 attacks have unwittingly ensured that their extremist cause will be discredited among many of their sympathizers, disowned by most of their former sponsors, and finally defeated by their enemies: two thousand years of the lessons of terror dictate that this is the ultimate fate that awaits the attackers, no matter how many noncombatants they manage to kill along the way. The pendulum of response now swings back to America, and the vital question becomes, In answering these attacks, can we control the temptation to enter into an equally gratuitous escalatory contest of not only weapons of *mass* destruction but weapons of *every* kind of destruction? In other words, is the United States right now in a position not to simply parade ever greater amounts of military and destructive muscle but to devise new forms of warfare that can be restricted in their effects yet decisive in their outcome?

The traditional American style of warfare ranks among the most hostile to ideas of creative limitation. America has generally relied, particularly since entering the industrial age and slogging its way through the Civil War, on overwhelming force and the debilitating power of attrition to reach its military goals. The few exceptions to this rule—most notably the American flirtation with blitzkrieg during the liberation of Europe in 1944–1945—took place despite the immense anxiety of the top-level commanders who oversaw them. Such a tradition would not seem to bode well for innovative solutions to the predicament at hand; yet the very gravity of that predicament will, almost certainly, dictate a departure from tradition. This is not an unknown phenomenon in military history. During the First World War, for example, none of the principal participants believed that they were entering into what would be a protracted contest; and when they found themselves facing just that, at least one power—Germany—underwent a period of profound confusion, for protracted wars of attrition did not conform to the German (which effectively meant the Prussian) tradition. The United States now finds itself in exactly the inverse position: the tactics that we have traditionally turned to in times of war—unlimited—must now be abandoned in favor of more precise, limited methods if we wish to emerge not only safe but once again living within the kind of stable international order that is required for the operation of international democratic capitalism. And we must jettison our traditional approach faster than did the Germans, lest we face the similar prospect of having to fight the same conflict a second time, after defeat has taught us how to conduct it appropriately.

The history of warfare against civilians has presented us with certain lessons from which we can illuminate principles that can guide us to a shift in our traditional behavior. Yet before we can even proceed to an examination of how to achieve a new variation on the kind of limited, progressive war that does not encompass deliberate assaults against noncombatants, it is necessary to decisively answer the question of whether the conflict in

which we find ourselves even qualifies *as* a war, or if we
are instead dealing with widespread international crimes
that are essentially forms of mass murder and as such are
the concern of law enforcement. For despite all the media
hysteria about "America's New War," there are still respected analysts who believe that we are faced with a
situation that is not precisely a state of belligerency. After
all, the argument can reasonably be made that many of
the incidents and conflicts from which the lessons in this
study have been drawn were declared international conflicts, whereas terrorism involves no open statement of hostilities, no formal declaration of war; so can we really say
that the lessons drawn herein apply to our current crisis?

It is vital in this context to recognize, however dis-
comforting the realization may be, that comparatively
few conflicts that we think of as wars have complied with
the nicety of legal notification of intent to commit military aggression. Certainly civil conflicts from the time of
Rome to our own war between the states and on through
the battle between North and South Vietnam have relied
on the commencement of hostilities rather than formal
declarations of war to announce and define them, as have
such colonial and imperial conflicts as the long and bitter
campaign by the United States to put down the Filipino
nationalist movement following the Spanish-American
War. Indeed, of the scores of conflicts in which America
has engaged in the last two and a quarter centuries, only

a few have been legally declared; and the rest of the world's record is no better. The most recent international effort that was generally thought of as and called a "war," the Persian Gulf conflict, involved a coalition but no formal declarations of hostilities. Based on such precedents, we can and must define war as a de facto state of hostile international relations, rather than a de jure or legalistic one. (Of course, it is always helpful and preferable to go into hostilities *with* such formal declarations of war, in order to avoid precisely the sorts of controversy and confusion that have surrounded our current use of military tribunals and the domestic detainment of foreign nationals; but the executive branch of the American government has traditionally avoided such declarations, which it views as limiting its freedom of action. This makes it all the more important to understand and define war as a de facto condition.) The distinction is important, for the recognition of a state of war takes operations out of the defensive and reactive (which are usually conducted by intelligence agencies and law enforcement) and widens them to include the kind of offensive and preemptive strategies on which, as we have seen, limited war depends for its success.

The second most common objection to defining the problem of international terrorism as war is the nature of the combatants themselves. It is true that international terrorists rarely wear the defining uniform or speak for the interests of one geographically circumscribed nation; yet in their own minds, they may speak for a great deal more. The members of such contemporary groups as Hezbollah, Islamic Jihad, and Al Qaeda believe themselves to be defenders of the "nation" or "kingdom" of Islam generally, and they certainly consider that kingdom to be at war with the United States. Nor is the "kingdom" of Islamic fundamentalism a new or confined phenomenon: the roots of what may fairly be called Muslim puritanism stretch back hundreds of years, past the Wahhabi movement of the eighteenth century to the ninth-century opposition to the scientific and artistic advances of the caliphate of al-Ma'mun. Clearly, this is not the modern, evolved form of some fringe group like the Assassins, a fact that is further attested to by the ability of radical fundamentalist Muslims to train militarily, organize an effective intelligence service, build a cell-based operative system that is remarkably difficult to crack, and master the tools of the information revolution. We now know that the members of these organizations inhabit dozens of countries (including most of those in the West), that they number in at least the tens of thousands, and that they exist in a perpetual state of mobilization. As one Egyptian expert on the subject put it several years ago, "Fundamentalism is globalized. It is as globalized as the Sixth Fleet."

Such an enemy *must* be considered an army, whatever its failure to conform to the popular Western conception of such, or to recognize the regulations for the conduct of war established at the various Geneva conferences and at the United Nations. Similarly, the undeclared state of hostilities in which we find ourselves *must* be considered a war. To think anything else is not only to deny the present reality but to deny the entire course of military history. Thus, while arguments over what domestic law-enforcement measures are or are not constitutional can and indeed must continue, all quibbling over whether we are or are not at war with an army of soldiers must stop. We must turn our full attention to devising strategies that can better serve us than total war has over the past half century.

Some may raise the objection that we do not now live in a world that admits any possibility of limited, progressive war; indeed, given the nature of recent conflicts, such a conclusion is understandable. Brutality, massacres, terrorism, and even genocide have become daily facts of international life: ours is not a moment that would seem to resemble any of the heydays of limited war. The eighteenth-century Western Enlightenment, for example, was an age that valued true creativity and a humanistic approach in all disciplines of thought—as did its greatest military thinker, Frederick the Great. The Italian Renaissance, which gave us the *condottieri,* was also such an age, as was the English Renaissance, out of which emerged Francis Drake and the other privateers who wrote an end to the regressive, brutal power of the Spanish empire.

Yet not all seminal military advances have occurred during cultivated, felicitous eras: the English civil war came hard on the heels of the Thirty Years War and the wars of the Reformation and was itself influenced by questions of religion—hardly a moment when one would expect to encounter such important military progress as was embodied in Oliver Cromwell's New Model Army. And the military doctrine that wrote an end to the static horror of trench warfare, blitzkrieg, was formulated to a decisive extent by men living in interwar Germany: initially one of the most hopeless environments of modern times and later one of the most barbaric. Then, too, while such periods as the Enlightenment may have been conducive to progress in the West, they were times of unlimited conflict and religious intolerance in other regions, such as Arabia. Thus, when we ask ourselves whether the admittedly savage dawn of the twenty-first century (with its wars of unprecedentedly univeral scope) or the United States of the same era (with its libertarian but vulgar, open yet exploitative society) are venues in which new and progressive military ideas might thrive, we can not only answer that they *must* be, for the sake of world stability and the advancement of civilization, we can also confidently assert that true military creativity is not dependent on the events or values of the moment. It hinges only on whether a given nation has the will to find and pursue such ideas, and, just as important, whether those ideas will serve the interests of that nation effectively enough to make them practical.

If we assume that the United States has both the will and the opportunity to pursue a progressive course, what will such a war resemble? The first principle of responding to unlimited warfare against civilians is, as we have observed, *not* to respond with similar behavior. This may, on the surface, sound like a simple enough idea, but it has proved to be one of the most stubborn problems in all of American military history, especially during the last century. And there has been no more persistent cause of this difficulty than the undying American belief in the decisive strategic effect of long-range destruction, particularly bombing campaigns. Having failed to learn from the failure of strategic bombing to destroy the enemy's will in both the Second World War and Vietnam, the American air force once again went to the strategic-bombing formula not only during the Gulf War but during subsequent air campaigns in the Balkans, as well as during the various cruise-missile strikes (which are improved but still problematic versions of higher-altitude strategic bombing) that were launched against Iraq, Afghanistan, and Sudan during the 1990s. In all of these campaigns, civilian damage and loss of life varied in severity, but it was always present, and it always bred resentment and even hatred, not only among enemy civilians but among such victims of collateral damage as the Chinese, who saw their embassy in Belgrade bombed (reportedly due to a CIA mapping error) in May 1999. The American air force has tried to dress up the dismal record of strategic bombing, of course, through the usual tactic employed by generals to defend a beloved tactic or weapons system: they have misrepresented events, as certainly as Hermann Goering, in 1940–1941, misrepresented the state of the British people as being one of near capitulation, owing to the German air bombardment.

A particularly pointed example of this American misrepresentation is the case of the "coalition" bombing campaign (which was actually, as usual, primarily a British and American operation) that preceded the ground operations of Operation Desert Storm. One of the main objectives of that campaign was the destruction of Iraq's facilities that produced weapons of mass destruction. (This was also one of the real priorities of the war itself, however much President George H. W. Bush may have painted the campaign as one undertaken to free the invaded nation of Kuwait.) After launching countless sorties, the Pentagon declared that it had in fact curtailed or even disabled Iraqi leader Saddam Hussein's ability to produce such weapons, and that the capacity to achieve such results from the air alone heralded what it called "a revolution in military affairs." Yet the international coalition had taken so long to array itself against Iraq that Saddam had had more than ample opportunity to hide and relocate much of his most important equipment. Three biological-weapons facilities were not even touched by the weeks of coalition bombing (which may have been fortunate, since attacks on chemical and biological facilities from the air always run the risk of dispersing the agents contained inside them; whatever the claims of the U.S. Air Force, such operations can be safely undertaken only by ground troops). Of Iraq's nuclear facilities, those that were successfully hit had been largely stripped of their crucial components. Saddam's centrifuge program, furthermore, a central part of his nuclear quest, was left unscathed. The American air force could display pictures of damaged buildings all it liked, but subsequent UN inspections of Iraqi nuclear- and biological-weapons facilities indicated that the damage to actual equipment, rather than buildings, was far less than the half-truths told by the Pentagon had led Americans to believe.

Nor was this the only time at which, or the only way in which, Pentagon spokespersons created a misperception among the American public concerning the coalition bombing campaign. Following the commencement of ground actions, huge numbers of Iraqi soldiers deserted to the coalition forces; during subsequent press conferences, the Pentagon painted a picture of hardened troops, such as Saddam's prized Republican Guard, reduced to quivering masses. Subsequent interrogations of Iraqi prisoners by the media, however, indicated that many of them had simply been waiting for the commencement of ground action so that they would have someone to whom they *could* surrender. In other words, they had not been so much traumatized by the air campaign as they had tried to last it out. The intention to desert was already there, but the air forces could still claim that the defections were their doing.

But of course, the single most tragic result of the air campaign, as well as the periodic air strikes and cruise-missile raids that were undertaken in the years that followed, was the transformation of the Iraqi people from an ambivalent population trying to survive the rule of a ruthless dictator into a much more anti-Western— and specifically anti-American—nation. Rarely in recent history has the real effect of strategic bombing been so clearly revealed: it *galvanizes* rather than breaks a people, and although in Iraq this effect was also assisted by the economic embargo that endured after the coalition forces had departed, it was initiated by the faceless destruction that has always been and remains strategic bombing.

Of course, such galvanization can take different forms. In the Balkans, one such different form gave the Clinton administration and the Pentagon additional ammunition with which to trumpet the idea that wars can be won from the sky alone. The 1999 bombing of Belgrade was eventually punctuated by the Yugoslav people's ejection of Slobodan Milošević, following elections that

Milošević tried but failed to nullify. Again, a coincidence of timing opened the way for inflated air-force claims: there had been extended bombing; Milošević had then been voted out of power; therefore Milošević's exit was the result of that extended bombing. But as in the Iraqi case, various preexisting or additional factors were not publicly acknowledged. Internal considerations and conditions that contributed to Milošević's downfall—including an educated and determined opposition—were simply ignored, as was the withdrawal of Russian support, along with a more ominous development: the growth of anti-American sentiment during and following the bombing campaign. Presumably, if the air strikes had been the sole instrument of Yugoslav liberation, the Yugoslavs would have demonstrated widespread gratitude for the help; they most certainly did not. But neither of these facts fit into the worldview that the Clinton administration (which carried on an eight-year love affair with strategic bombing) and the Pentagon (which was happy to play on Clinton's lack of understanding and deep dread of full-scale military operations) were trying to promote. Appearances, as always with Clinton, were what mattered; and Milošević's fall could be made to look like the result of air strikes alone.

Such attempts to use and portray long-range bombardment as a decisive strategic instrument, beyond being of extremely questionable morality, are always counterproductive. Therefore, abandonment of such tactics—or at least their demotion to a very circumscribed support role—would fit the two criteria for progressive war: it would stop the diminution of American and Western moral authority that has already reached a disastrous point and would at the same time serve our military and national-security interests.

Yet if strategic airpower is to be thus curtailed, surely some other flying weapons must take a primary role: the skies cannot simply be abandoned to enemy aircraft and terrorist hijackers. This is of course true. But the kind of airpower that the United States today requires is that which can guarantee genuine precision, which comes not from high altitudes but from low, not from laser guidance but from human guidance. On the obvious level, this means enhancing our tactical air units; fighter-bombers, as well as attack and support helicopters, along with such versatile and high-impact weapons as the AC-130, the propeller-driven plane that is loaded with so much tactical weaponry that it is in effect flying artillery.

Yet there is an even more innovative military aircraft that has only recently begun to play a crucial role in operations, particularly in Afghanistan: the RQ-1A Predator, a long-endurance, medium-altitude unmanned aircraft that is relatively small and was originally intended for reconnaissance and surveillance missions but can now be fitted with explosive payloads. When so modified, the

Predators can become a modern army's answer to the suicide bomber: the Predator is remote-controlled and thus governed by human intelligence rather than strictly by a computer, as is the case with cruise missiles. It carries real-time, on-demand video reconnaissance equipment—in effect, "eyes"—with which it can relay six separate points of view to a mobile control truck located almost anywhere, making it capable of discrimination. Its choices of target become its operator's choices of target, and civilian casualties can therefore be much more effectively limited. It is also highly useful against the kind of tactical, handheld (or, as the military vocabulary now has it, "man-held") weapons that terrorists use heavily, such as shoulder-launched missiles, because it is pilotless and its loss involves no casualties. The Predator aircraft could be one of the salient weapons of a postmodern military, and one can only hope that its production, and that of remote-guided yet discriminatory weapons like it, has already been drastically increased, much as tank production in the United States was increased after Pearl Harbor. For this is a weapon that also fulfills the criteria of limitation and progressiveness: a curbing of civilian casualties, as well as the advancement of our national-security interests through an augmented ability to strike offensively and decisively.

There are many additional steps that can be taken to enhance our moral authority and serve our national interests; but perhaps none would have greater meaning to the many countries that want better relations with America yet cannot tolerate its often arrogant interference in their internal affairs than the limitation and finally the elimination of covert operations by American intelligence agencies, particularly the CIA. It is a guiding principle of the fight against terrorism not to adopt terror's methods, yet the CIA has not only practiced them, it has instructed other nations and groups in their use. This avid, almost orgiastic acceptance and implementation of what James Doolittle called a "fundamentally repugnant philosophy"—in other words, the willingness to fight a dirty enemy with dirty methods—has been the closest American emulation of the Roman policy toward barbarian leaders and warriors. Similar policies did much damage on many occasions to the early Islamic empire and later to the British empire. Unless checked soon, it may well become for America what it was for Rome, for Britain, and for the Muslims: a central cause of collapse.

Indeed, Osama bin Laden can easily be seen as America's own Arminius, the German tribal chieftain whose fiery indictments of Roman military arrogance and religious idolatry inspired the German tribes to rebellion during the reign of Augustus. As is now well-known, bin Laden is a product of that height of CIA folly, the training, arming, and sponsorship of the Afghan *mujahidin* prior to and during the Soviet occupation of Afghanistan

in the 1980s. The CIA had long demonstrated a willingness to associate itself with and actively assist questionable groups of all authoritarian and reactionary varieties,
so long as they were anticommunist; but the *mujahidin*
represented a new low. A collection of fanatical Muslim
fundamentalists without equal in their enforcement of
strict Koranic law, the *mujahidin* incorporated into their
military tactics and social "policies" traditional Afghan
tribal customs ranging from horrific torture and execution methods to playing polo with the heads and bodies
of prisoners. But they were tenacious fighters and offered
first the Carter and then the Reagan administration the
chance for what was rather childishly and ignorantly perceived as "revenge" against the Soviets for Vietnam.
Jimmy Carter's national-security adviser, Zbigniew Brzezinski, has often crowed, in print and on television, about
his pride at having assisted in drawing the Russians into
the battle for Afghanistan, control of which had been a
desire of Moscow's for centuries. At least one U.S.
Congressman, displaying the popular American miscon-
ception that the Soviets had choreographed the North
Vietnamese resistance, gave open voice to widespread
feeling that "we owe the Russians one" and that "the Soviets ought to get a dose of it."

But as blind, ugly, and extensive as was the CIA's
sponsorship of the anti-Soviet Islamic Afghan forces (who
were quickly dubbed "freedom fighters" by the Reagan

administration in 1981, though the only freedom that many if not most *mujahidin* desired was the freedom to torture, steal, and rape), it was the behavior of the Agency *after* the battle against Russia had been won that was most colossally irresponsible. By simply abandoning the *mujahidin* with nothing but the Stinger missiles and other weapons with which they had armed them, the CIA ensured civil conflict and famine in war-ravaged Afghanistan for years to come, as well as resentment so powerful that it turned especially the younger Muslims against the United States; and among that younger group was a wealthy Saudi volunteer named Osama bin Laden.

Had this operation been an aberration, or even had its sordid and unpleasant outcome been unusual, one might not be led to such a stern judgment of the Agency's behavior. But the Afghan experience was in keeping with every experience in the CIA's pre- and post-Vietnam records. We have seen the depths to which the Agency was capable of sinking before 1975; yet even the withdrawal from Saigon did not humble or chasten it. Not only did it enter into a dozen other schemes like the sponsorship of the *mujahidin* (particularly in Central America, during the widespread strife and disorder that affected six of those seven nations during the 1970s and 1980s), but it continued to fail in the performance of its primary duty of analyzing world events and predicting developments of truly major significance. Indeed, in a bizarre bit of irony, the CIA, which for its entire existence had rationalized any questionable operation or the sponsorship of any questionable leader on the basis of their being anti-Soviet, did not understand the Soviet Union well enough to predict its downfall. In the late 1980s, the Agency was still reporting that Moscow represented a strong and vital threat to American national security. It is safe to say that no one was more surprised by the rapid sequence of events that led to the Soviet collapse than the arrogant, operations-happy denizens of Langley, Virginia.

The CIA has, over the years, opened the United States to an unprecedented array of criticism, which has run the gamut from sophomoric left-wing protests at home to angry—indeed, bloodthirsty—indictments abroad. For many years, more sober and responsible analysts of both the American intelligence establishment and American national security have, upon studying the Agency's cost/benefit ratio, determined that America would be far better off if the Agency were abolished. America possesses extraordinary intelligence redundancy: the CIA's field-research operations could be folded into such established programs as the FBI's international division, while the job of analyzing such intelligence has always been done better by the National Security Agency and other intelligence arms, which at least have managed to keep *some* of their attention focused on the full international picture.

It would be difficult to imagine a move that would

send a more powerful signal to other countries that the United States intends to change the way it does global business than abolishing the CIA. But this should not even be a consideration unless it would heighten rather than diminish American national security. And we can quickly see that it would, first by putting other intelligence agencies on notice that they are also expendable and had better start doing their investigation, research, and analysis jobs better than they were done prior to the September 11 attacks, and second by closing those avenues of threat that the questionable loyalties of certain key CIA operatives have kept open. Few agencies have hurt American interests by employing traitors more than the CIA; indeed, as has been seen in cases such as that of the confessed double agent Aldrich Ames, the Agency may have sent more vital information out of the United States than it has brought in.

And what of the operational activities that have been the CIA's obsession? Under a radically new arrangement, these could be left to those units most qualified to undertake them: not civilians playing at war games, but actual soldiers, specifically tasked units of America's underdeveloped special forces. Indeed, the evolution of American special forces from auxiliary divisions of the existent services (SEALs in the navy, elite airborne units in the army) into a fifth spoke in the wheel of American military might could well be the most important single aspect of any revamping of the American military and national-security structure that is focused on the ability to fight limited wars that are strategically decisive. At no time during the post-Vietnam era has the dominance of special-forces operations, and especially tactics, suggested to any senior officers or officials in Washington that the special forces have graduated from an auxiliary role (just as the marines did long ago) and therefore deserve to be treated independently, with their own academy, their own budget, their own chief of staff (or commandant), and their own secretary. This would elevate special forces past the status of "elite" troops, to be used only in extreme situations, into that of a new kind of regular soldiers in a new kind of war. In such a war, where it is far more difficult to separate combatants from noncombatants, troops with greater tactical discrimination are not only advisable but required.

As with most such seemingly technical or bureaucratic moves, there is a moral dimension to such an elevation of America's special forces. For the assignment of covert operations to CIA agents who are improperly trained and ultimately as unaccountable as their organization has, as said, not only opened America to a broad range of criticism but badly corroded the perception of America as a just nation. The CIA, in other words, has been living proof of "Vattel's law": the manner in which a country chooses to conduct operations is the real measure of the validity of that country's cause. How else could a nation

that has been by far the most generous in history—
particularly since the Second World War—have come to
be viewed as being in the wrong so often? Some analysts
say that this is the natural result of being the only great
power: the inevitable danger of hegemon status. Still others chalk it up to envy, saying that other countries simply
want what America has and hold America rather than
themselves responsible for their inability to get it. There is
some truth in each of these points, but neither explains
adequately the extent of the hostility toward America in
today's world. It is therefore time to apply Vattel's law to
ourselves as vigorously as we have been willing to apply it
to others, in order to not only construct a superior military establishment but to better attend to the ethical
(which in this area become the practical) requirements of
progressive war: for progressive war is, again, the only
kind of war with which terrorism can truly be eradicated.

In setting specific objectives for this new, more progressive military machine, we must revisit a question
that has plagued American generals and policymakers
throughout the post–Second World War era but particularly in the last twenty years: whom exactly, in a given
struggle, are we fighting against? This is not simply a military question, although it is certainly that; for the purposes of maintaining public support as well as of limiting
the impact on civilians, clarity of war aims is essential.
Lately, however, it has eluded the United States on many

occasions. We have from time to time been told, for example, that the United States does not make war on individuals. Indeed, this was the stated reason for our failure (and failure it was) to march on Baghdad during the Gulf War and put an end to Saddam Hussein's brutal regime, once his army had been defeated in the field. And yet the coalition forces that had entered Iraq had already been careful to announce, as had our political leaders, that we were not at war with the Iraqi people. This presented a logical dilemma, one that was carefully and consistently sidestepped by American and coalition leaders: if we do not make war on individuals, but we were not at war with the Iraqi people, then whom precisely *were* we at war with? The answer generally given was that the coalition had moved against Saddam's forces to expel them from Kuwait and undo the Iraqi occupation; but such a goal is not a practical or effective military objective. A nation cannot go to war with an action such as a military occupation, for to do so puts that action in a class with natural disasters such as earthquakes and hurricanes. An invasion or a genocide or a terrorist attack is the work of *human beings,* and if it is not a *nation* of human beings that is responsible for that work then it must be an *individual* or a *group of individuals,* and those individuals must be brought to justice that is summary, not criminal, since the process that they have initiated is war.

This confusion over the precise identity of the enemy

or enemies in the Gulf War contributed heavily to the toll
among noncombatants, for it meant not only that the
Iraqi people were heavily bombed but that they were left,
after the coalition's departure, in the grip of a powerful
authoritarian regime that many of them had opposed
(thinking that the coalition would support them). It also
meant that Saddam Hussein's dangerous behavior would
continue, necessitating the imposition of economic sanc-
tions that did nothing to erode his power but did spread
privation and death among the Iraqi people. Fear was
voiced at the time that Iraq might collapse into civil war
if Saddam was removed. But once Iraq's capacity to produce weapons of mass destruction had been definitely
eliminated (as, again, it could only have been from the
ground) could such a civil conflict possibly have had a
worse effect on either the Iraqi people or Western interests than Saddam's ongoing domestic and international
campaigns of terror?

We can see this need to more precisely understand and
define war aims—to further limit war—demonstrated
when we contrast the failure in the Persian Gulf with two
of America's more successful military operations of recent
times: the tactical air attack on Libya in 1986 and the invasion of Panama in 1989. Both these actions had clear
objectives, and they were similar. Libya's head of state,
Muammar Qaddafi, was a longtime terrorist sponsor who
the Reagan administration—badly scarred by such terror-

ist acts as the 1983 bombing of a marine barracks in Beirut—believed had played a key facilitating role in almost every major terrorist attack of the preceding decade or more, most recently the bombing of a German nightclub that American soldiers had been known to frequent. The aim of the 1986 raid was to strike key Libyan military installations, but only as a cover for the larger purpose: to kill Qaddafi or, at the very least, to so terrorize *him* that he would forsake the sponsorship of terror. Qaddafi did not die during the attack, though he was badly shaken; and although he did not altogether give up his terrorist activities in the years to come (he may or may not have played a role in the downing of Pan Am flight 103), they became dramatically less frequent.

In the case of Panama, the purpose outlined and the action taken were even more forthright. General Manuel Noriega, the Panamanian dictator who had once been a CIA operative (another of the Agency's modern triumphs), had turned on the United States, which of course has always had anxieties about the canal that it long ago built but agreed under President Jimmy Carter to transfer to Panama by the end of the century. President George H. W. Bush was a former director of the CIA and thus had good reason to know how unstable and unpredictable Noriega was. The Panamanian leader's personal behavior, along with that of his infamous defense forces, was rapidly promoting a state of violent anarchy. And so,

in 1989 the United States invaded Panama, captured
Noriega, and brought him to the United States for trial.
The legalistic conclusion of the episode perhaps clouded
its record a bit, but no more than that: American leaders
had clearly and realistically decided that although they were
not at war with the Panamanian people, they *were* most
certainly at war with the Panamanian leader (though it
was a war that was, again, never declared), and they
openly went about the business of nullifying him.

The same group of American leaders would have done
well to follow the same strategy in Iraq just over a year
later. Instead, they returned to the strategic rules for the
commitment of American troops that had been laid out
half a decade earlier by Ronald Reagan's secretary of defense, Caspar Weinberger, in what became known as "the
Weinberger doctrine." These guidelines had laid out six
basic prerequisites for action, all of which had a deceptively simplistic, even obvious, ring to them: first, the
"engagement" should be "vital to our national interest";
second, America should have "the clear intention of winning"; third, the military and political objectives should
be "clearly defined"; fourth, those objectives must be
"continually reassessed and adjusted"; fifth, the undertaking must "have the support of the American people and
their elected representatives in Congress"; and finally,
military action should be only "a last resort."

The Weinberger doctrine had a profound effect on an

already hesitant and conservative Pentagon bureaucracy that preferred its grotesquely inflated peacetime budgets to the active defense of American interests; and its overall air of cautiousness would be reinforced by President Bush's chairman of the Joint Chiefs of Staff, Colin Powell, who emphasized restraint rather than exercise as the most impressive aspect of military power (an idea he reportedly borrowed from Thucydides) and insisted on assembling (but not, in keeping with the first thought, necessarily using) overwhelming military force prior to a campaign.

Both of these doctrines stood at great odds with all historical notions of limited, progressive warfare. Weinberger's nod to "clearly defined" objectives was deceptive, for there were, it turned out, only certain "clear definitions" that he was willing to consider, and their common bias was the same as the general prejudice of his doctrine: extreme caution. The overall philosophy of the Weinberger doctrine and the Powell corollaries was seemingly in keeping with the American military tradition of overwhelming force and attrition in the pursuit of an absolute or unconditional objective; but it soon became apparent that, next to Weinberger and Powell, Ulysses Grant looked like a wild-eyed gambler. For Grant, much as he did depend on overwhelming force and attrition, and much as he was willing to sacrifice tens of thousands of lives to both principles, did at least do *something* politically decisive with his overwhelming force. In addition, he was, on occasion, at least willing to authorize (for he was himself incapable of authoring) such daring strategic concepts as Sherman's march through Georgia and the Carolinas. Weinberger proved to have difficulty with similarly adventurous concepts; it was up to Reagan's secretary of state, George Shultz, to be the member of the cabinet who most actively promoted a vigorous, offensive, and preemptory acceptance of challenges to American security—especially that of international terrorism.

In a speech made just before Weinberger promulgated his doctrine (a speech, indeed, that may have egged Weinberger to rebuttal), Shultz asked, "Can we as a country, can the community of free nations, stand in a purely defensive posture and absorb the blows dealt by terrorists? I think not. From a practical standpoint, a purely passive defense does not provide enough of a deterrent to terrorism and the states that sponsor it. It is time to think long, hard, and seriously about more active means of defense—defense through appropriate preventive or preemptive actions against terrorist groups *before* they strike." Here at last, after more than two hundred years of unlimited war, was an American call to observe the principles of limited, progressive war, principles that were embodied in the raid on Libya two years later. During that action, not only were civilian casualties—and indeed the scope of operations generally—kept to a minimum, but the means deployed were tactical rather than strategic (for the reward of surprise was rightly considered worth the gamble), and the objective was both clear and deadly, as was the message: continue to sponsor terror, and we will use perpetual diligence and preemptory offensive force to hunt you down and, if possible, kill you. Assassination of rebel leaders, it will be remembered, was one of the most effective Roman policies for quelling uprisings, far more effective than large-scale punitive war. Today, we should bear that lesson in mind and remember that terror's *only* effective, legitimate use is against military personnel and heads of state (the latter becoming, in times of war, supreme commanders, and therefore military as well as civilian leaders). Shultz certainly convinced his president—as well as Libya's—of as much: with a comparative handful of tactical aircraft, the Reagan administration was able to produce a more profoundly inhibiting effect on Qaddafi than Bush and Powell would effect on Saddam Hussein with an armada and an expeditionary force.

There are other aspects of the Libya raid that must be kept in mind when formulating future responses, not only to terrorism but to all military threats. The American government never established Qaddafi's personal responsibility for any terrorist act in a manner that would have stood up in criminal court; the attack on Libyan territory therefore represented not a direct assault on terrorists per se but on their state sponsors. As we have learned lately—all *too* late—the conventional military forces of such state sponsors must be considered, in effect, terrorist auxiliaries, and not purely for military reasons. By attacking the conventional forces of state sponsors, we drastically change the position of those states in their regional balances of power; and if we have learned one thing about even committed terrorist states, it is that, much as they may hate America, they value their regional power even more. This was one of the reasons the 1986 raid had such a profound effect on Qaddafi, who is by no means an easily frightened man: he recognized that the loss of his conventional forces meant the diminution of his status as a regional player. And that proved to be almost as intolerable an eventuality as death. This is an effect we must, when necessary, be willing to re-create with other state sponsors of terrorism, for it is a policy that is in keeping with progressive war's emphasis on the offensive and surprise.

The final element of the 1986 raid that must be underscored is that in embarking on it, the United States paid strict observance to UN Article 51 (which permits military action in self-defense) but to nothing else. There was no attempt to build a coalition against Qaddafi, which would only have served the same purpose it later did in Iraq and, more recently, in Afghanistan: to alert the enemy that an attack was coming. Indeed, in the Libya operation the French government, when consulted, refused to allow U.S. fighter-bombers that flew from England to cross their nation's airspace; the chances of building a coalition would likely have been slim. But the American planes persevered, factoring in the time it would take to fly around pusillanimous France and launching early enough to make their strikes. The lesson here is one that is essential to the achievement of surprise, or at times to the simple avoidance of disaster. We must remember that in 1950, when he received word that North Korea had invaded South Korea, President Harry Truman, taking the advice of his secretary of state, Dean Acheson, launched American planes in response *before* UN approval had been obtained, which it eventually was. (The Organization of American States, on the other hand, which similarly received no advance warning of the U.S. invasion of Panama, was "outraged" when it received the news; unlike the UN in the case of the Koreas, however, it stayed that way.) The military initiative, as well as the occasional need to avoid military disaster, does not function according to the timetables of coalitions. If our endeavors demand that we act alone, then we must do so.

Is there a way to build on the philosophy to which Shultz gave voice in 1984 but that was first confused and interrupted by the Weinberger camp, then further inhibited (despite the success of the Libya raid) by the more operationally conservative members of the Bush administration, and finally was killed off by the utterly incompetent military undertakings of the Clinton administration?

Some of the specific methods have been outlined above, but there is a more fundamental piece missing here, one that the current secretary of defense, Donald Rumsfeld, has attempted—with considerable success—to supply. It is the promulgation of an overall military philosophy for a new kind of war: not simply an elaboration of weapons programs and strategic and tactical concepts but an ethical evocation that approaches the teachings of Frederick the Great and Vattel. For, again, we are at a point in history that is of no less magnitude than was theirs. Vattel is particularly important in this regard, because of his recognition of one central truth: military reform cannot be imposed by outside moralists and legalists, no matter how well-intentioned (as in the case of St. Augustine) or brilliant (as in the case of Grotius). Rather, military reform must grow organically from the principle of military and political self-interest: the greatness of "Vattel's law" lies in its inherent recognition that no nation obeys external moral castigations. If a reform will not advance national interests, a nation will not undertake it. Therefore it is now up to military thinkers—historians, theorists, and officers—to devise methods of uniting the acceptance of progressive war (and the attendant abandonment of total war) with the vigorous pursuit of American national security. The history of warfare provides ample proof that such unity is indeed possible; it is simply laziness, dull-wittedness, and a taste for destruction and vengeance that cause so many armies, factions, and individuals to forgo it.

We stand now, obviously, at a crossroads: not only a crossroads concerning which direction our military development will take but a crossroads concerning the future of civilization. There have never been two more vital and powerful forces at work in the world than international capitalist democracy and fundamentalist Islam, nor two forces more capable of physical and cultural destruction: of differing types of warfare against civilians. In the years to come, both sides will need to formulate and inform their behavior with philosophies that reflect an understanding of their own as well as each other's excesses and commit to genuine programs of reform. Islam must finally reinterpret those contextual, anachronistic passages of the Koran that were so necessary to the survival of the faith in seventh- and eighth-century Arabia but that now propel men to self-defeating acts of terror against civilians. Similarly, evangelical Western capitalism must learn greater restraint and respect for other cultures, and Western governments, specifically the American, must finally acknowledge that the days of gunboat diplomacy are over and that such behavior is itself terribly self-defeating. Our armed forces must be designed and employed for the protection of the American people, not of American business (which, indeed, behaves in a far less rampant, far more responsible fashion when it does not assume that it enjoys military protection overseas). In 1815, an aging Thomas Jefferson went straight to the heart of this point when he asked a friend "whether profit or preservation is the first interest of a state?"

It may be difficult for many to accept that military reform—philosophical as well as organizational—can play such an enormous role in social transformation; yet the lessons of terror attest to this truth and light the way along the only path that represents enlightened belligerent action. Those lights have been similarly lit for many other nations and several other global hegemons, who have chosen to ignore them and to wander in the darkness that is unlimited war. In our own case, there will certainly continue to be voices that will try to dissuade us from those most essential principles of progressive war: refusal to target civilians, constant offensive readiness, the ability to achieve surprise, an emphasis on discriminatory tactical operations, and the strength to act alone, if necessary, in order to vigorously attend to our security. Such strategies, tactics, and policies have been confirmed by two thousand years of hard experience, experience that must finally overcome prevarication that passes for caution. Surely we have the wisdom to respect the efforts and the sacrifices that have been made during those centuries, as well as enough self-interest and charity to lead not only our nation but our world out of its current crisis, and steer it clear of similar calamities in the future.

SELECTED BIBLIOGRAPHY:
GENERAL SOURCES

Adams, James. *Engines of War.* New York: Atlantic Monthly Press, 1990.

Aquinas, Thomas. *Selected Writings.* London: Penguin Books, 1998.

Ashley, Maurice. *The Greatness of Oliver Cromwell.* London: Collier-Macmillan, 1957.

Asprey, Robert B. *War in the Shadows.* Garden City, N.Y.: Doubleday, 1975.

Augustine, Saint. *City of God.* New York: Doubleday, 1958; London: Penguin Books, 1970.

Bamford, James. *The Puzzle Palace.* New York: Penguin Books, 1983.

Blum, William. *Killing Hope.* Monroe, Me.: Common Courage, 1995.

Brzezinski, Zbigniew. *Power and Principle.* New York: Farrar, Straus, and Giroux, 1983.

Bury, J. B. *The Invasion of Europe by the Barbarians.* New York: Norton, 1967.

Chace, James, and Caleb Carr. *America Invulnerable.* New York: Summit Books, 1988.

Childs, John. *Warfare in the Seventeenth Century.* London: Cassell, 2001.

Clausewitz, Karl von, and Sun Tzu. *The Book of War:* On War *and* The Art of Warfare. New York: Modern Library, 2000.

Cordingly, David. *Under the Black Flag.* New York: Random House, 1995.

Cowell, F. R. *Cicero and the Roman Republic.* London: Penguin Books, 1964.

Dawood, N. J., trans. *The Koran.* London: Penguin Books, 2000.

Earle, Edward Mead. *Makes of Modern Strategy.* Princeton: Princeton University Press, 1943.

Erasmus. *In Praise of Folly.* London: Penguin Books, 1993.

Ferrill, Arthur. *The Origins of War.* London: Thames and Hudson, 1985.

France, John. *Western Warfare in the Age of the Crusades.* Ithaca, N.Y.: Cornell University Press, 1999.

Fuller, J.F.C. *The Conduct of War, 1789–1961.* New Brunswick, N.J.: Rutgers University Press, 1961.

———. *Grant and Lee.* Bloomington: Indiana University Press, 1957.

———. *A Military History of the Western World.* New York: Da Capo Press, 1987.

Goldsworthy, Adrian. *Roman Warfare.* London: Cassell, 2000.

Graebner, Norman, ed. *The National Security.* New York: Oxford University Press, 1986.

Guillaume, Alfred. *Islam.* London: Penguin Books, 1969.

Hallam, Elizabeth, ed. *Chronicles of the Crusades.* New York: Weidenfeld and Nicolson, 1989.

Hitti, Philip K. *Makers of Arab History.* New York: Harper, 1971.

Hobbes, Thomas. *Leviathan, Parts One and Two.* Indianapolis: Bobbs-Merrill, 1958.

Johnson, Loch K. *America's Secret Power.* Oxford: Oxford University Press, 1989.

Josephus. *The Jewish War.* London: Penguin Books, 1981.

Kaplan, Robert. *The Coming Anarchy.* New York: Random House, 2000.

Keen, Maurice. *Chivalry.* New Haven: Yale University Press, 1984.

Keen, Maurice, ed. *Medieval Warfare.* Oxford: Oxford University Press, 1999.

Kessler, Ronald. *Inside the CIA.* New York: Pocket Books, 1992.

Kimche, Jon. *The Second Arab Awakening.* New York: Holt, Rinehart, and Winston, 1970.

Kissinger, Henry. *Diplomacy.* New York: Simon and Schuster, 1994.

Laqueur, Walter. *The New Terrorism.* Oxford: Oxford University Press, 1999.

Lesser, Ian O., et al. *Countering the New Terrorism.* Santa Monica: Rand, 1999.

Liddell Hart, B. H. *Strategy.* New York: Praeger, 1967.

Livy. *The War with Hannibal.* London: Penguin Books, 1965.

Lord, Walter. *The Dawn's Early Light.* New York: W. W. Norton, 1972.

Matthias, Willard C. *America's Strategic Blunders.* University Park, Pa.: Pennsylvania State University Press, 2001.

Millis, Walter, ed. *The Forrestal Diaries.* New York: Viking, 1951.

Netanyahu, Benjamin. *Fighting Terrorism.* New York: Farrar, Straus, and Giroux, 1995.

Netanyahu, Benjamin, ed. *Terrorism: How the West Can Win.* New York: Farrar, Straus, and Giroux, 1986.

Nutting, Anthony. *The Arabs.* New York: New American Library, 1964.

O'Toole, G.J.A. *Honorable Treachery.* New York: Atlantic Monthly Press, 1991.

Pancake, John S. *This Destructive War.* Tuscaloosa: University of Alabama Press, 1985.

Parry, Albert. *Terrorism from Robespierre to Arafat.* New York: Vanguard, 1976.

Rhodehamel, John, ed. *The American Revolution: Writings.* New York: Library of America, 2001.

Royster, Charles. *The Destructive War.* New York: Vintage, 1993.

Seton-Watson, R. W. *Britain in Europe, 1789–1914.* Cambridge: Cambridge University Press, 1945.

Sherman, William Tecumseh. *Memoirs.* New York: Library of America, 1990.

Stern, Jessica. *The Ultimate Terrorists.* Cambridge, Mass.: Harvard University Press, 1999.

Suetonius. *The Twelve Caesars.* London: Penguin Books, 1957.

Tacitus. *The Annals of Imperial Rome.* Dorset Books, 1984.

Vattel, Emmerich de. *The Law of Nations.* William S. Hein, 1995.

Woodward, Bob. *The Commanders.* New York: Simon and Schuster, 1991.

Yergin, Daniel. *Shattered Peace.* London: Penguin Books, 1990.

INDEX

ABOUT THE AUTHOR

CALEB CARR, a military historian and novelist, is a contributing editor of *MHQ: The Quarterly Journal of Military History* and the series editor of the Modern Library War Series. He was educated at Kenyon College and New York University and is a former employee of the Council on Foreign Relations in New York. His military and political writings have appeared in numerous magazines and periodicals, among them *The World Policy Journal, The New York Times, Time,* and the *Los Angeles Times.* He currently lives in upstate New York.

ABOUT THE TYPE

This book was set in Garamond, a typeface designed by the French printer Jean Jannon. It is styled after Garamond's original models. The face is dignified and is light but without fragile lines. The italic is modeled after a font of Granjon, which was probably cut in the middle of the sixteenth century.